Garden
Heroes
and
Villains

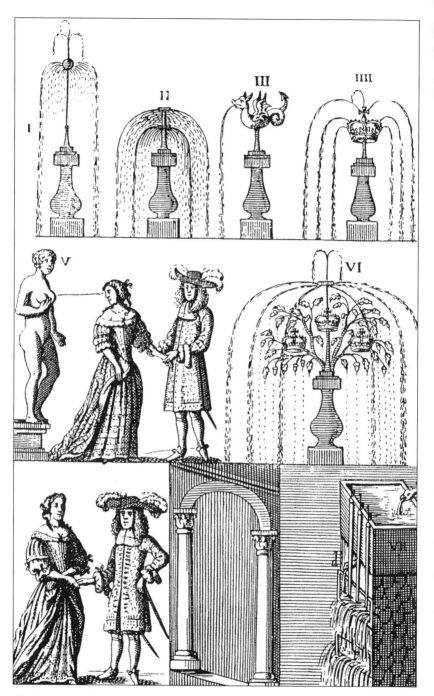

Joke fountains in Italian Renaissance gardens. (Worlidge, *The Art of Gardening*, 1688)

Garden
Heroes
and
Villains

GEORGE
DROWER

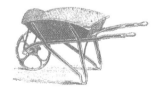

SUTTON PUBLISHING

First published in 2006 by
Sutton Publishing Limited · Phoenix Mill
Thrupp · Stroud · Gloucestershire · GL5 2BU

British Library Cataloguing in Publication Data
A catalogue record for this book is available from the British Library.

ISBN 0 7509 3366 6

Typeset in 11/14pt Photina.
Typesetting and origination by
Sutton Publishing Limited.
Printed and bound in England by
J.H. Haynes & Co. Ltd, Sparkford.

Contents

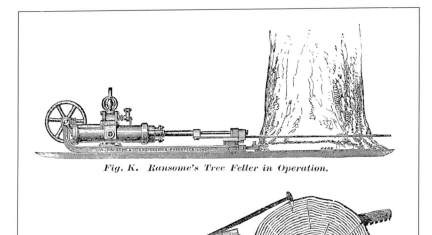

Fig. K. Ransome's Tree Feller in Operation.

Fig. L. Ransome's Tree Feller as a Cross-cut.

A steam saw. (Grimshaw, *Saws*, Remsen and Haffelfinger, 1880)

Introduction

Most gardeners have needed to become familiar with those mischievous and worryingly widespread plants such as Japanese knotweed, giant hogweed, and common rhododendron. But what of the villains who, perhaps unwittingly, introduced them? Who were they and what caused them to bring them here? Then there are those really useful practical garden features such as timber decking, lawn rollers and greenhouses: who was it who devised them?

In surprisingly many respects it has been characters beyond the immediate world of horticulture – whether environmentalists, founders of institutions, engineers, scientists, financiers or entrepreneurs – who have influenced the content and shape of gardens. Some contraptions and ideas have been especially relevant to certain forms of garden: containers and ingenious window-sill devices for city roof terraces; timber decking and peat compost grown for town gardens; lawnmowers and gnomes in the suburbs; and cattle grids and ha-has for country estates. So who were these unsung heroes and demonic villains? How did their ideas come about?

Among the heroes who devised ingenious tools, particularly significant was Edwin Budding, a Gloucestershire mechanic who innovatively rotated a bench-mounted cloth-trimming machine by 90 degrees to create the world's first lawnmower. Hitherto lawns had to be cut by teams of mowers using scythes, which meant they were the preserve of the wealthy. Budding's brilliantly simple machine changed all by enabling millions of middle-class gardeners to quickly mow their own lawns – although many who dislike cutting lawns might claim he was the villain who created the summer weekend drudgery of having to keep such green spaces neat. Another machine that seemed to evolve from an earlier function was the chainsaw. Originally invented in 1785 by John Aitken, a Scottish surgeon, to cut through bones during operations, it was not developed for the purpose of cutting trees until 1929, when it was put to use in forestry work by a German industrialist called Andreas Stihl, and has since become infamous – especially abroad – as a device by which woodlands have been destroyed.

Then there were good-natured enablers, like the socialite Elsie Wagg, whose simple adjustment of an existing idea radically transformed gardens and gardening. In 1926 her suggestion to the owners of country houses that they might like to fleetingly open their hitherto unseen grand gardens to the public was an instant success. Not only did the idea achieve its objective of providing charitable financial assistance to district nurses, it allowed people to visit gardens on an organised basis, and later saw the creation of the 'Yellow Book' National Gardens Scheme. Earlier, in 1913, the distinguished nurseryman Sir Harry Veitch advocated the use of the grounds of the Royal Hospital at Chelsea to provide a regular venue for the Royal Horticultural Society (RHS)'s annual outdoor flower show in central London. The relocation greatly improved the popularity of the annual show, thereby enabling thousands more people to view some of the best products of British horticulture.

The motives causing garden heroes and villains to behave as they did varied considerably. Surprisingly, one of the most powerful was jealousy. In 1894 the Chancellor of the Exchequer, Sir William

Harcourt, devised a punitive tax which became known as death duty. Harcourt had been envious of his elder brother who was to inherit the family's country estate and a place in the House of Lords, while he himself had, following Gladstone's resignation, just been pipped for the top post of prime minister by Lord Rosebery. The long-term consequence, over several decades, of Harcourt's tax was the destruction of hundreds of country houses and their gardens. Unexpectedly however, it had the beneficial effect of spurring the establishment of the National Trust; and it also eventually caused the Harcourt dynasty to lose its main country house. Another vengeful garden villain was Cardinal Ippolito d'Este, who built a magnificent garden near Rome to rival that of Pope Julius III (after he had been outmanoeuvred from becoming pope himself in 1550). His garden at the Villa d'Este influenced the building of garden fountains throughout Europe, with splendid designs derived from the ancient models of Heron of Alexandria.

Love them or loath them, gnomes were introduced into Britain through the Northamptonshire country estate of Sir Charles Isham, a well-meaning, reclusive baronet who never envisaged they would escape into so many suburban gardens. Then there was the rash of timber decking spurred by TV makeover programmes in recent years, and which has been much criticised for unduly dominating gardens at the expense of planting. In fact, decking was first perfected in the 1930s by Thomas Church, one of the United States's most prestigious landscape architects. Church advocated timber decking as a stylish means to protect trees and plants – though he was insistent that it should only be done when it accorded with the existing garden.

Some heroically struggled to change prevailing opinions. John Rose did just that in 1665 when he insisted that vines could be successfully grown in England. Horticultural journalism, which until the 1820s had preponderantly been concerned with descriptions of plants, was revolutionised by John Claudius Loudon's illustrated magazine's encouragement of ingenious mechanical contraptions for suburban gardens. Then in the 1950s Lawrence Hills influentially campaigned to urge gardeners to grow produce using organic methods. The insecticide DDT, invented by Nobel Prize winner Paul Muller, was widely used in gardens until banned because of compelling observations made by the environmentalist Rachel Carson concerning its dangers to wildlife.

Thus garden heroes and villains varied from the unknown to the famous. In fact, as in real life, not only was it often the most unlikely persons who were the real heroes and villains, but they frequently became so almost by accident. At times the improvers' intentions were selflessly altruistic, and sometimes garden heroes and villains influenced the appearance of gardens far beyond their own lifetimes. And, fortunately, the villains usually gave rise to saviours, and, in the long run, good often prevailed over evil.

1

Techno Wizards

Ferrabee Lawnmower. (*Gardeners' Chronicle,* 1852)

Edwin Budding's Lawnmower

In August 1830 a patent was filed for a grass-cutting contraption that was so revolutionary it would eventually enable virtually anyone to have an immaculate lawn. Hitherto, the absence of an effective mechanical means of cutting grass had meant that lawns had been the exclusive preserve of the privileged. For landowners who favoured a more systematic method than allowing livestock to nibble their green patches, lawn-cutting was usually done with a scythe, a primitive implement with a crescent-shaped blade that was swished to and fro on a long curved wooden handle.

Scything was quite a skill, as the social commentator William Cobbett noted: 'A good short-grass mower is a really able workman.' However, because grass could be cut only when heavy with damp, the hapless operatives had to work either in the early morning dew, or in the rain, or, occasionally and most grimly, at night by the light of torches or the moon – at the risk of horrendous personal injuries. As J.B. Papworth's 1823 *Hints on Ornamental Gardening* noted, even sleeping householders were not immune from the fortnightly lawn scything procedure because of the mowers' frequent use of sharpening stones to hone their blades, 'generally at the time of the morning when such noises are most tormenting'! And yet, irrespective of the mower's dexterity when using those fearsome cutters, the scythe unavoidably left many circular scars and unsightly irregular surfaces.

The only available cutting means other than the scythe was hand-shears, which were used at the edges of lawns and where the grass was too short or inaccessible under bushes. By advocating an enlarged version of that simple device, a Scottish landscape painter called Alexander Nasmyth (1758–1840) dabbled at making the first mechanical grass-cutter. In the late eighteenth century Nasmyth ingeniously suggested cutting horticultural grass with a pair of 6ft-long shears. Unfortunately, his gigantic spring-loaded scissors worked only on seriously overgrown lawns and were so heavy and cumbersome that they had to be trundled about on a wheel!

The seemingly improbable venue of the really significant breakthrough in the development of lawn-cutting equipment was the bustling mill town of Stroud, which in the early nineteenth century was the hub of the Gloucestershire woollen industry, astride several converging valleys. The district had ambitions to improve its prosperity by enhancing its reputation as maker of smooth quality woollen products, and to facilitate this a race was on to find a means of cutting the rough imperfections and knotted blemishes (called 'naps') from the surface of its finished cloth. In 1815 the clothier John Lewis in the local village of Brimscombe reckoned he had solved the problem by means of a bench-mounted machine with a cylinder of rotating blades into which the cloth was fed. The cut was uneven, however, because the blades struck the cutting plate at intervals, but within weeks that important cropping difficulty was solved by Stephen Price. A Stroud engineer, Price was reputedly inspired by a napping machine that was invented in America (by someone called Mallory) and then imported to a local mill. In August 1815 Price patented a machine similar to Lewis's except that the blades on the cylinders were curved, thus providing a continuous cut.

Nasmyth's early mower consisted of a pair of gigantic hand shears. (Stuart, *Georgian Gardens*, Robert Hale, 1979)

Price's device was apparently made at the Phoenix Mill foundry in Stroud and installed in numerous mills in the neighbouring valleys. At the nearby town of Dursley the machines were serviced by Edwin (Edward) Beard Budding, a technician who has since been variously described as a mechanic, foreman and carpenter.

Budding had an aptitude for solving engineering problems, and already had the beginnings of a track record as the inventor of a variety of devices. Between 1825 and 1830 he designed a revolver that was more advanced than Samuel Colt's patent of 1836. Later on he would also design an adjustable wrench and a lathe. Quite when he had the brainwave of wondering if the napping contraption could be adapted into being an effective means to cut grass is unclear, but that he did is beyond doubt.

Unlike so many seeking to profit from their innovations, Budding had the business nous not to be too greedy. Wisely reckoning he could best advance himself by sharing his discovery, in 1830 he went into business partnership with John Ferrabee, who had established the Phoenix Iron Works in 1828 and developed a reputation for producing quality engineering contraptions. By an agreement signed on 18 May 1830 their profits from the lawnmower were to be equally divided. John Ferrabee, who undertook to finance the cost of the revolutionary grass-cutter's development, would have the right to manufacture, sell and license other manufacturers to produce lawnmowers. Edwin Budding's responsibility would be to solve any technical difficulties in the lawnmower's production.

Historically, although Budding came to be accepted as the *inventor* of the lawnmower, in his historic 1830 'Machine for Mowing Lawns' patent, he very deliberately admitted that his device was essentially an *innovation*: 'I do not claim as my Invention the separate parts of my machine, considered without reference to the effects to be produced by them; but I do claim as my Invention the described application and combination for the specified purpose.' Unlike Price's bench-mounted napping device, which needed to be driven by crank wheel or belt from a revolving waterwheel, the lawnmower was supposed to be pushed (although

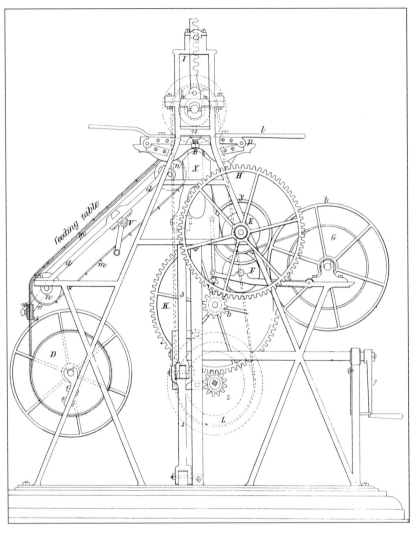

Price's 1815 cloth shearing machine, which Edwin Budding innovated by rotating it through 90 degrees to convert into a lawnmower! (Patent Office, 1815)

a second handle was provided so that, if required, it could also be pulled). In 1831 the prototype was made by Ferrabee to Budding's design. The mower had a main roller that drove the whirling knives through a system of gears, which enabled those 19in cutting blades to rotate at twelve times the speed of the roller, and worked against a rigid knife bar on the underside of the machine.

The Budding lawnmower went on sale in 1832 at a cost of 7 guineas, which included a grass box and wooden packing case (the manufacturer's catalogue also offered package and delivery 'to any principal railway station in the United Kingdom'). Technically brilliant though Edwin Budding might have been, he was also commercially minded enough to allow his radical new machine to be presented as being enormously fun to use. Thus, conspicuous in the otherwise dour wordage of his 1830 mower patent, were the encouraging words: 'Country gentlemen may find in using my machine themselves an amusing, useful, and healthy exercise.' In 1831 one of the very earliest mowers went into service at the Zoological Gardens in Regent's Park. According to an enthusiastic article in the *Gardener's Magazine* soon afterwards, the foreman, Mr Curtis, claimed to be entirely delighted with the machine which 'does as much work as six or eight men with scythes and brooms . . . performing the whole so perfectly as not to leave a mark of any kind'.

However, the operational reality was that the cast-iron lawnmower was so heavy, that when covering large areas it often took two persons to cut with it. Other practical difficulties were that the cutting cylinder immediately at the front of the machine was so close to the ground that sometimes it would (contrary to the London Zoo's glowing endorsement) catch mounds on the surface and lurch the machine into the ground, thus leaving an

Budding's revolutionary 1830 lawnmower patent. (Patent Office, 1830)

Budding's Machine for cropping or shearing Grass Plats &c.

FIG. 1. AN ELEVATION.

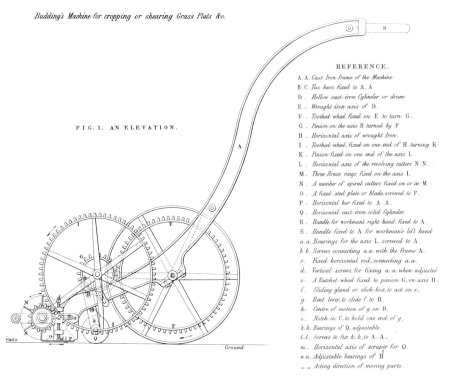

REFERENCE.

A.A. *Cast Iron frame of the Machine*
B.C. *Two bars fixed to* A.A
D. *Hollow cast-iron Cylinder or drum*
E. *Wrought-iron axis of* D.
F. *Toothed wheel fixed on* E *to turn* G.
G. *Pinion on the axis* H *turned by* F
H. *Horizontal axis of wrought Iron.*
I. *Toothed-wheel, fixed on one end of* H *turning* K.
K. *Pinion fixed on one end of the axis* L.
L. *Horizontal axis of the revolving cutters* N.N.
M. *Three Brass rings fixed on the axis* L.
N. *A number of spiral cutters fixed on or in* M
O. *A fixed steel plate or blade, screwed to* P.
P. *Horizontal bar fixed to* A.A.
Q. *Horizontal cast-iron solid Cylinder.*
R. *Handle for workman's right hand, fixed to* A.
S. *Handle fixed to* A *for workman's left hand*
a.a. *Bearings for the axis* L *screwed to* A.
b.b. *Screws connecting* a.a. *with the frame* A.
c. *Fixed horizontal rod, connecting* a.a.
d. *Vertical screws, for fixing* a.a. *when adjusted*
e. *A Ratchet-wheel fixed to pinion* G, *on axis* H.
f. *Sliding gland or click-box, to act on* e,
g. *Bent lever, to slide* f, *to* H.
h. *Centre of motion of* g, *on* B,
i. *Notch in* C. *to hold one end of* g,
k.k. *Bearings of* Q, *adjustable.*
l.l. *Screws to fix* k.k. *to* A.A.
m. *Horizontal axis of scraper for* Q
n.n. *Adjustable bearings of* H
← *Acting direction of moving parts.*

FIG. 2. A PLAN.

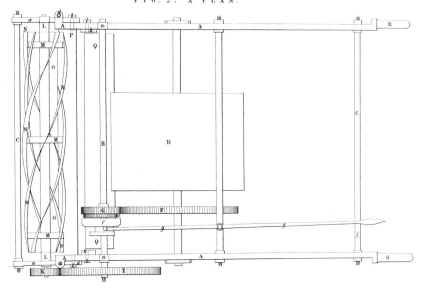

BUDDING'S

PATENT

Machine for cutting Grass Plats, &c.

SOLD, BY APPOINTMENT, BY

J. R. & A. RANSOME,

IPSWICH.

This Machine is so easy to manage, that persons unpractised in the Art of Mowing, may cut the Grass on Lawns, Pleasure Grounds, and Bowling Greens, with ease. It is easily adjusted to cut to any length; and the beauty of its operation is, that it leaves no seam, nor any of the cut grass upon the Lawn. Other advantages of this Machine are, that the grass may be cut when dry, and consequently it may be used at such hours as are most convenient to the Gardener or Workman,—while the expence of Mowing is considerably lessened, as more than double the work may be done with the same manual labour that is requisite with the Scythe.

8. Advertisement for Budding's grass cutter, as made by J. R. & A. Ransome, 1844 (P1/A 102).

Budding and Ferrabee produced the lawnmower themselves and also licensed its manufacture to other machinery makers, such as Ransomes of Ipswich, who produced this advertisement in 1844. (D.R. Grace and D. Phillips, *Ransomes of Ipswich*, University of Reading, 1975)

8

uneven height of cut; and the contraption had an exposed cogwheel drive which made it extremely noisy. According to the *Gardener's Magazine*, 'so great was the noise caused by these cogwheel machines, that in most establishments they could not be used while the family was in residence before 8am, when the inmates had risen'. So not much improvement from the scythe!

Ferrabee soon realised that, although his own selling network was well established, he needed to reach a wider market. In 1832 Ransomes of Ipswich, already renowned as manufacturers of plough shares and other agricultural machinery, were sold a licence to produce and wholesale the Budding mower. Another licensee was James Shanks, a Scottish engineer in Arbroath. When a Budding lawnmower purchased to cut the 2½ acres of lawns on the wealthy W.F. Carnegie's Arbroath estate was found to be not up to the job, Shanks was asked to build a 27in-wide mower that could be pulled by two horticultural labourers, or a pony. The latter proved to be the most effective when cutting was carried out in dry weather, since the pony left no hoof marks on the grass and enabled Carnegie to cut his lawns in less than three hours. In 1842 Shanks registered the design in Scotland of an even larger such machine, 42in wide (the term 'shanks's pony' reputedly originated from this innovation). Budding's patent only covered England and Wales, because until 1852 Scotland still had its own patent regulations. Nonetheless, in 1841 Ferrabee had travelled to Scotland to check with Shanks that there were no infringements. The use of animal power was established and some horticultural firms even began selling leather galoshes to protect lawns from damage by the ponies' hooves.

Regardless of the practical usefulness of Budding's radical machine, sales were such that by the early 1850s a total of only

For several decades, Budding's simple lawnmower shape – a cutting cylinder supported by large and small rollers – remained the standard format for all mowers, including these 1842 shanks's pony mowers advertised on the lawn at Balmoral. (Sanecki, *Old Garden Tools*, Shire, 1979)

some 4,000 mowers had been sold. This was partly because the mower was still too far ahead of its time: the idea of suburban lawns had still not really caught on; nor had the explosion of enthusiasm for sports played on grass, such as lawn tennis, cricket, golf and football. Also, the hitherto innovative Budding inexplicably seems to have made virtually no attempt to improve on his original design. During the 1830s he and Ferrabee had merely extended their product range with 16in and

22in machines, and then 30in and 36in devices in 1852. But now there was a sense of desperation because the Patent Office had started to allow improvements in design to be patented, which opened up the field to others. Thus, even though Budding's simple 'penny-farthing' chassis format would remain the mainstay of popular lawnmower design, it would be others who would find the solutions to the significant improvements that needed to be made.

It was Ransomes of Ipswich, for example, who solved the problem of the revolving cutting cylinder colliding with the ground. Having realised the fault was a matter of imbalance caused by the small wooden roller behind the cutting cylinder being too close to the rear drive roller, Ransomes placed the cylinder between the rollers – a brilliantly simple solution that led to an even cut. In terms of the lawnmower's irritatingly noisy gears, Budding had proffered the cure in his 1830 patent, which stated: 'The revolving parts may be made to be driven by endless lines, or bands, instead of teeth.' Astonishingly, nothing was done about this until 1859, when Thomas Green, a Leeds blacksmith, patented the world's first chain-driven lawnmower. This too had a conventional 'penny-farthing' chassis, but compared to the Budding gear-drive mowers was virtually noiseless. New forms of propulsion were then applied. In 1892 James Sumner of the Leyland Steam Motor Company produced the first ever steam-powered mower, although it did nothing to solve the lawnmower weight problem, because it weighed 1½ tons! Seven years later Ransome's patented the first ever petrol-driven lawnmower, a cumbersome 42in contraption ideal for sports fields.

By then had appeared a machine that offered amateur gardeners an affordable means of mowing. In 1869 Budding's penny-farthing format was superseded by the Manchester firm

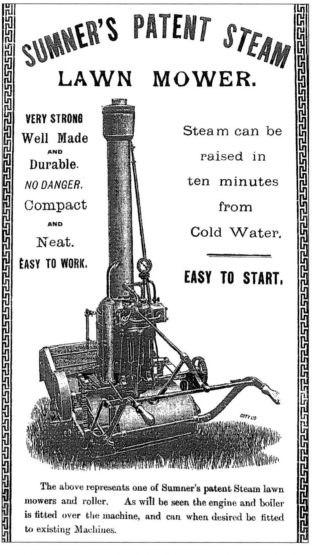

SUMNER'S PATENT STEAM LAWN MOWER.

VERY STRONG

Well Made

AND

Durable.

NO DANGER.

Compact

AND

Neat.

EASY TO WORK.

Steam can be

raised in

ten minutes

from

Cold Water.

EASY TO START.

The above represents one of Sumner's patent Steam lawn mowers and roller.   As will be seen the engine and boiler is fitted over the machine, and can when desired be fitted to existing Machines.

In the 1890s Sumner's invented a steam mower weighing 1½ tons! (Halford, *Old Lawnmowers*, Shire, 1982)

James Sharp's Metal Roller

Before the invention of the lawnmower, unsightly scars on lawns, caused by cutting with a scythe, had to be smoothed over with a heavy roller. The early rollers were mostly made from tree sections attached to 'A'-shaped frames of timber, or even wrought-iron. The disadvantage of wooden rollers was that they were susceptible to rot and their symmetrical shape could become uneven. The only alternative was to use stone rollers, which, though heavy and better suited to crushing gravel paths, were durable. Nevertheless, no matter how well the early wooden and stone rollers were made, they all suffered from being awkward to steer. All that changed in 1773 when the horticultural machine supplier James Sharp devised a divided roller. At his premises in the City of London's Leadenhall Street, Sharp began making and selling the revolutionary all cast-iron contraptions which had two – and sometimes three or more – rollers. With the cylinders revolving independently, the entire roller was now far easier to turn. Some of Sharp's rollers had a brake mechanism in the form of a simple counterweighted arm, which, when released, would swing vertically and make the roller stationary.

Iron rollers invented and sold by James Sharp in the 1770s had: (a) divided rollers for better steering, and (b) counterweighted arms for easier moving and braking. (James Sharp, *Descriptions of Some Utensils*, London, 1773)

A Divided Garden Roller with Ballances

Made & Sold by James Sharp London

Follows and Bates, who devised a patent mower known as the Climax. Instead of having an extremely heavy main roller, that device cleverly had two large, though lightweight, outside side wheels with internal cogs, through which the cutting cylinder was driven. This meant that the machine had few parts and was therefore much lighter. It sold for virtually a fraction of the old Budding machines: compact, 6in-wide mowers ideal for cottage gardeners could be bought for 10*s* 6*d*. Appropriately, because the side-wheelers were especially effective on coarse grass, they sold exceedingly well to gardeners in America – from where, ironically, the idea for the inspirational cloth-napping machine might have originated.

Sadly, Edwin Budding never lived to see the numerous variations of his ingenious machine in popular use. In 1846 he died of a stroke, aged only 50. The lawnmower, it seems, did not make him wealthy, nor did it warrant his receiving an obituary or any form of visual portrait. In his later years, although a trusted partner at the Phoenix Iron Works, he eked out a living at the nearby town of Dursley as an engineer at Lister's, successfully working to improve the perpetual carding machine, which had inspired his original lawnmower idea. Subsequently, and despite his position as a garden hero, he was also seen as something of a villain because it was his lawnmower that created the tyranny of all gardeners being obliged to be seen to have tidy lawns.

Original Budding lawnmowers can be seen at the Stroud Museum, www.stroud.gov.uk and Old Lawnmower Club, Milton Keynes, www.oldlawnmowerclub.co.uk. See also the British Lawnmower Museum, www.lawnmowerworld.co.uk.

John Aitken's Chainsaw

Now the most destructive and controversial horticultural tool – tainted by involvement in the destruction of rainforests – the chainsaw is often assumed to have been invented in the 1920s by a German engineer called Andreas Stihl. It was, in fact, originally devised in the late eighteenth century as a medical instrument!

Its creator was John Aitken, an Edinburgh surgeon who lectured on chemistry, anatomy, medicine and surgery at the University of Edinburgh. Of his early life not much is known other than that he probably learnt his trade in Edinburgh and published books on medical subjects, such as *Principles of Midwifery or Puerperal Medicine* (1784). It sold at a price of *2s 6d*, and the good-hearted doctor donated the proceeds to an Edinburgh maternity hospital he had founded in 1784. Then followed *A System of Obstetrical Tables with Explanations* (1786). It was in these works that Dr Aitken outlined and illustrated devices

John Aitken, the eighteenth-century Scottish surgeon who invented the chainsaw. Because his device evolved into a tree-cutting machine he unwittingly became a villain. (The Wellcome Trust)

for use in obstetrics. One, which he invented himself, was the chain or 'flexible' saw. Before the introduction of this device, surgeons operating on bones had needed to use a scalpel or conventional medical saw, which all too often unavoidably caused considerable collateral damage to tissue and organs around the bone that required sawing.

Aitken's saw consisted of two handles connected by a serrated steel chain (like a miniature bicycle chain) with sharp teeth cutting on the convex surface. The cutting contraption was introduced by means of a curved needle passed through the soft tissue around the bone. When the saw was in position the needle was replaced by a handle, and then the second handle was attached. The device would then be pulled back and forth around the bone to be cut off. Use of the chainsaws meant there tended to be less need for limb amputation, which at the time was standard treatment for severely infected and damaged bones. Almost simultaneous (in 1786) another Scottish doctor, James Jeffray, who was a surgeon in Glasgow, apparently invented a remarkably similar saw, except that his was modelled on a watch chain. In 1876 Tieman & Company, a firm of medical instrument-makers, patented a saw consisting of two handles connected by a wire of cast steel on which were strung a series of steel beads with sharp cutting edges. Nevertheless, for much of the nineteenth century, Aitken's simple chainsaw was a useful surgical instrument which seemed to require no modification.

The next evolutionary step in chainsaw evolution occurred forty-six years after John Aitken's death in 1790. In 1830 a German doctor of orthopaedics called Bernard Heine invented the first mechanical mechanism for a chainsaw. His 'Osteotome' consisted of angle-set cutting teeth attached to an endless chain that was guided by a blade around two sprockets driven by a

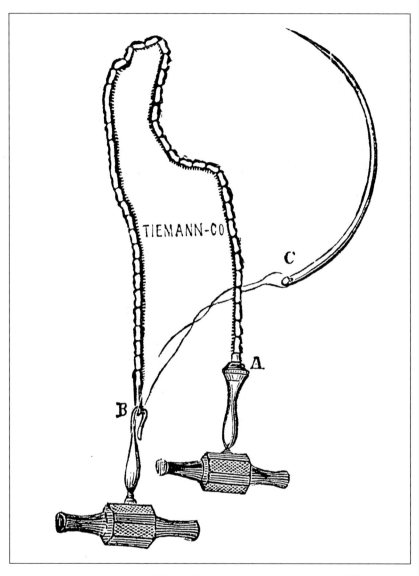

Medical chainsaw similar to Aitken's 1785 invention. (Grimshaw, *Saws*, Remsen and Haffelfinger, 1880)

handle on one of the sprockets. The device was said to be an improvement when performing amputations because it sometimes avoided the need to use a hammer and chisel. But the speed of the hand gearing was low and the saw ricocheted off compact bone, thus making it difficult to control. However, it made Heine a medical celebrity and in 1834 won him the coveted Prix Montyon of the Académie des Sciences in Paris. In 1894 the 'Osteotome' was improved on by Leonardo Gigli, an Italian obstetrician who introduced a fine twisted wire saw, which provided a narrower and quicker cut.

Surprisingly, it was quite a while before thought was given to adapting this medical technology for forestry work. Although thoughts of pre-chain-saw cutting equipment are likely to be of chopping down trees with axes, various forms of saw had been in use for a considerable time. The sturdiest of these was the crosscut 'ripsaw', which was introduced into Britain by the Romans for cutting planks and beams, and required two men to operate it. By the nineteenth century the crosscut saw was the generally preferred device for felling trees over 1ft in diameter. It was regarded as being more effective than the bowsaw with a wooden

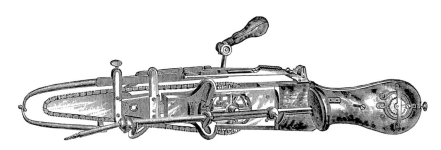

Chainsaws were used for surgery in the nineteenth century. (Grimshaw, *Saws*, Remsen and Haffelfinger, 1880)

frame, which though commonplace in that century, was too heavy, since the blades had to be wide and thick because they could not be tensioned.

In 1777 Samuel Miller invented the first circular saw, a round metal disk that had to be table-mounted – being immobile, it could not be taken into woodlands. The Hamilton saw, invented in 1861, was hand-cranked and resembled a spinning wheel. Yet that also was too cumbersome to be effective. Another promising development ought to have been the bandsaw, which was invented in 1808. Consisting of a flexible band of metal edged with teeth it was rotated between large leather-covered pulleys on a bench. However, the construction of the blades offered a paradoxical problem: they had to be soft and flexible to pass readily around the pulleys at a light speed, without breaking; and yet they also had to be sufficiently hard to receive and maintain a keen cutting edge, and stiff enough to resist the pushing tendency of a high feed. It was many decades before a strong enough blade for the bandsaw was invented, and when it was it could not cope with really thick wood, nor did it have the mobility to be operable in forests.

Attention then focused on adding some mechanical advantage to conventional reciprocating saws. The most technically advanced of these was the 'Steam Tree-Felling Machine' made by Ransome & Co. Essentially this was a railway-type piston connected by pipes to a boiler and mounted on an adjustable sledge to enable it to cut trees at ground level, or crosscut large sections of felled timber. Unfortunately, when tested by British foresters in a teak plantation in Burma in 1883 the machine went horribly wrong. In 1894 James Brown noted in *The Forester* the difficulty in generating a high pressure of steam, and because the saw strained in gripping the tree, it several times bounced about, risking serious accidents to the operatives.

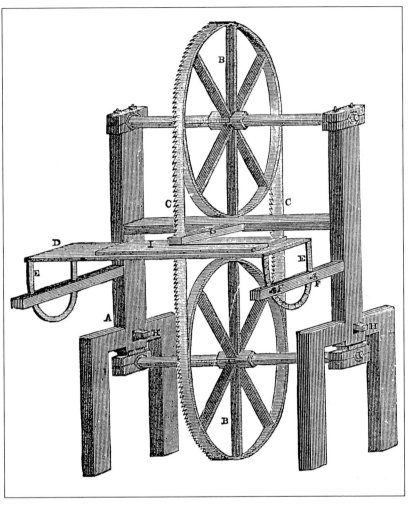

Original bandsaw of 1808. (Grimshaw, *Saws*, Remsen and Haffelfinger, 1880)

Patents issued at the Patent Office in London in the years before the 1930s show that even then inventors were struggling to devise contraptions that could cut forest timber efficiently. In 1925 J.T. Pickles advised using a bandsaw machine on a U-shaped frame; in 1909 J.H. Pattenden suggested a reciprocating saw machine supported by giant springs attached to portable stands; E.J. Pepper in 1916 tried to solve the problem of mobility and lightness by recommending a reciprocating device pivoted on a

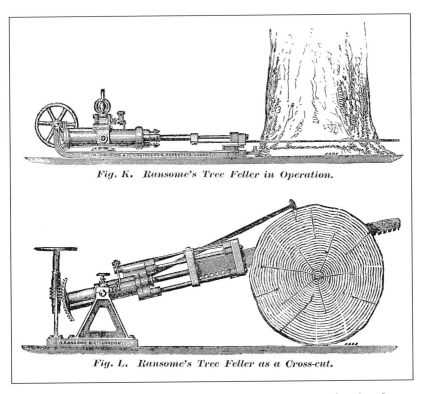

Fig. K. Ransome's Tree Feller in Operation.

Fig. L. Ransome's Tree Feller as a Cross-cut.

Before the invention of chainsaws, trees were sometimes cut by steam saws. (Grimshaw, *Saws*, Remsen and Haffelfinger, 1880)

tractor; in 1917 A. Holmberg's solution was a reciprocating saw powered by a petrol motor on a cart; while in 1911 Agar, Cross & Co. wanted to put a circular saw on a swinging frame attached to a steam tractor, and in 1919 suggested a circular saw on a tracked vehicle.

So far there was still no one who had sought to apply Aitken's bone-cutting tool to the work of slicing up wood. The Californian inventor R.L. Muir might have been the first person to put blades on a chain and thus invent the first chainsaw for logging purposes, but his invention, weighing hundreds of pounds, was not a commercial success. The eventual populariser of the hand-held mobile chainsaw was the German mechanical engineer Andreas Stihl, the founder of a company for making boiler pre-firing systems. In 1926 Stihl patented the 'Cutoff Chain Saw for Electric Power'. Then in 1929 he patented a petrol-engined, hand-held, 'tree-felling machine' – which weighed 101lb! At the time he made no attempt to acknowledge the prior technology of medical

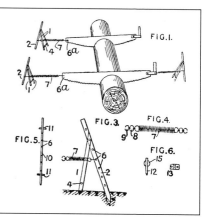

18,790. Pattenden, J. H. Aug. 16.

Reciprocating-saw machines. — Cross-cut and like saws are supported at each end by springs attached to portable stands constructed of cast or wrought iron bars 1, 2 bolted together at their upper ends. The side bars 1 are stayed by a cross-bar 4, and the rear bar 2 is pointed to engage the ground. Holes 6 are provided in the rear bar 2 to which the spring may be attached. The steel spring 7 is plain or rubber-coated, and is provided at each end with a swivel ring 8 and with a cross hook 9 or a catch for engagement with the holes 6, 6ᵃ. The spring may be composed entirely of rubber. In cases where a stand cannot be used, the spring may be connected to an arm 10 having projections 11 for engaging any suitable projection, or to the ring 15 of a spike 12 which is engaged with an eye-piece 13 secured to a stack of timber.

Pattenden's 1909 sawing machine. (Patent Office)

This 14lb machine made by Stihl Industries in 1967 was the first lightweight timber-cutting chainsaw, and remarkably similar in appearance to the hand-operated surgical devices evolved during the nineteenth century from Dr Aitken's original invention. (Bell, *Fifty Years of Garden Machinery*, Farming Press, 1995)

chainsaws. His Stuttgart-based company went on to become the first European firm to export chainsaws to America and Russia. In 1931 he produced a much improved, light and powerful 2-cycle 8hp motor for use by the German Army, which overcame the problem of so many early petrol saws – a weight disproportionate to the horsepower ratio. In 1950 Stihl developed the first chainsaw to be operated by one person. Nevertheless, it is remarkable that the first lightweight 5hp horticultural chainsaw, a 14lb model produced by Stihl in 1967, was so similar in appearance to the hand-operated surgical devices developed during the nineteenth century from Aitken's original invention.

A heroic labour-saving device though the chainsaw was to gardeners and professional woodmen, it became the *bête noire* of conservationists, who considered it to be a fiendishly inexpensive contraption used in developing countries to destroy ecologically valuable forests. The environmental madness of cutting, clearing and burning South American forests was spelt out as early as 1877 in *The Causes of Drought and the Necessity of Afforestation*, written by the Venezuelan engineer Julio Churion. His warnings went unheeded.

As for Dr John Aitken, he died in September 1790, apparently in an attack of delirium. His family's medical dynasty continued, however. When one of his descendants, who was also called Dr John Aitken, died in 1880, his appreciative patients in the Govan district of Glasgow, built a memorial in his memory – albeit of metal rather than wood.

There is a 1930s chain-link horticultural handsaw at the Museum of Garden History, Lambeth, London, www.museumofgardenhistory.org.

Heron of Alexandria's Fountains

The inventor whose water engines were so important in the making of sophisticated garden fountains was the ingenious Greek hydrologist Heron of Alexandria. Nevertheless, by the time his brilliant machines were eventually so influentially put into action at the infamous Villa d'Este, at Tivoli, they had in effect remained virtually undeveloped for some 1500 years!

Heron of Alexandria (AD 10–70) was a Greek engineer, mathematician and talented writer who was thought to have lived in Alexandria in about AD 62. By studying the works of earlier ancient scientists, and by doing some inventing himself, he became an authority on fundamental mechanical devices. His masterpiece treatise, *Mechanics*, is said to have been the first definitive practical work on the basic merits of pulleys, cogwheels, winches, screws and levers. Heron was a careful reader of Ctesibius (sometimes known as Ktesibious), a then deceased Greek engineer whose ideas on pneumatics and hydraulics Heron developed into sensible theories – also applying some of his own – which he expounded in two other significant treatises, *Pneumatica* and *Hydraulics*.

The Greeks' penchant for puppet theatre meant there was a market for elaborate show machinery. Heron catered for this in his work *Automata* by devising a moving stage which automatically moved in rectilinear or circular patterns for the duration of an entire theatre performance – all by means of ropes powered by the weight of falling sand. Heron developed such entertainment possibilities further by applying his understanding of the mechanical possibilities of multiple pulleys, cogwheels and levers to his knowledge of hydraulics and thereby devising intriguing

Heron of Alexandria. (Heron, *Buch von de Lufft-Unt Wasser Kunsten*, Frankfurt, 1688)

water engines. His *Pneumatica* disclosed the main examples of those schemes. Particularly ingenious was an owl fountain, which consisted of a group of artificial birds whose chirping was produced by water pressure and who fell silent whenever an owl turned towards them. Other clever ideas were for water-powered music organs, and trumpets sounded by compressed air. The inventions and innovations Heron made during his lifetime reputedly totalled nearly eighty and also included coin-operated vending machines, self-trimming lanterns, doors opened by lighting a fire, a form of milometer, a theodolite, formulas for calculating square roots of numbers and the area of a triangle, a theory of optics concerning beams of light, and the Aeolipile, a spinning heated sphere which effectively was the world's first steam engine!

Yet Heron and his written work containing details of his numerous contraptions and magical tricks were soon totally forgotten – except by the Arabs. Western Europe's knowledge of his output would have to wait several centuries, until partial representations began to appear, initially in the form of the Arabic *Book of Mechanical Devices* (1206) by Ibn al-Razzaz al Jazari of Diyarbakir. Some of that know-how might possibly have inspired the so-called 'pleasance' garden with spectacular water features constructed by Robert d'Artois in 1295 at Hesdin, in the Pas-de-Calais – horticultural features that were not well known of, even when the property was entirely destroyed in 1553.

However, between 1550 and 1572, in the hills near the Italian town of Tivoli, an astonishing Heron-derived Renaissance water garden was created, whose fountains became the most influential ever made. The garden's instigator was Cardinal Ippolito d'Este, who by virtue of his being the grandson of Pope Alexander VI, was a bishop at the age of 2, an archbishop when 10, and a

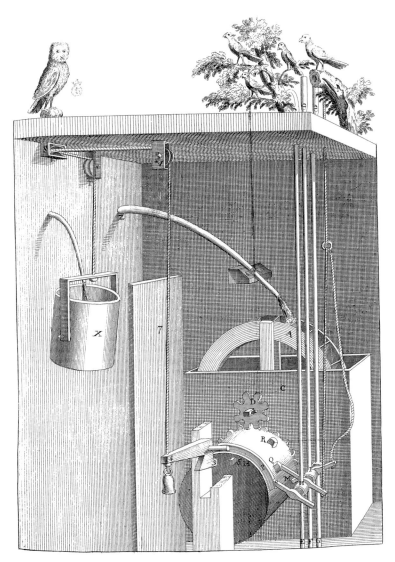

Heron's owl fountain. (S. Switzer, *An Introduction to a General System of Hydrostaticks and Hydraulicks*, Astley, 1729)

cardinal at 30. In February 1550, aged only 41, Ippolito nearly became pope, but in his quest to do so was outmanoeuvred by Julius III. A bitter rival, Julius III promptly made him a governor of Tivoli. It was a shrewd move. Tivoli was only 19 miles north-east of Rome, but because governors were forbidden to leave the provinces they ruled, Ippolito was effectively permanently exiled, remaining there for the last two decades of his life, plotting his revenge against Julius III and the papacy. His method was to establish at Villa d'Este a power garden as a deliberate object of envy and jealousy, where important visitors could also be made fun of. Curiously, those bitter sentiments were slightly out of character because, apart from his anger at Julius III, Ippolito was reportedly one of the most erudite, cultured, intelligent and discerning of artistic patrons. At the Villa d'Este these qualities helped him, as one of the wealthiest ecclesiastics of the sixteenth century, to create one of Europe's most spectacular gardens.

Villa d'Este, which was the name Ippolito gave to the site of his governor's palace, was formerly a monastery, which in turn had been built on the ruins of a Roman villa on a hill top on the edge of the town of Tivoli. South-west facing, it had views across the plain to Rome. To transform the property into an awesome showpiece Ippolito appointed the distinguished Naples architect, painter and writer Pirro Ligorio (1510–83). Fortuitously, Ligorio knew of Jerome Cardan's 1550 translation of much of Heron's *Pneumatica* and was highly knowledgeable about the antiquities of ancient Rome; he was also an antiques dealer who had recently become something of an expert on the vast ruins of the Villa Adriana. Built near Tivoli by the Emperor Hadrian (AD 76–138) and arranged around a long canal, the villa consisted of various fine buildings which reputedly had been supposed to represent different locations in the Roman Empire. In 1549 Ligorio began excavating the grounds of the villa in the search for antiquities. Ippolito reckoned that if statues and reliefs obtained from the Emperor Hadrian's villa could be incorporated into the house and garden at Villa d'Este this would be an additional kudos for him – at the expense of the popes in Rome.

Once certain local vineyards had been acquired to create an enormous site, building work eventually began in 1560 in accordance with a plan devised by Ligorio. To obtain a copious supply of water to feed the envisaged waterworks there, an aqueduct was constructed from the distant Monte Sant' Angelo River to bring water to the town of Tivoli and fill a large reservoir under the court of the monastery, and by cutting through the hills, additional water was brought from the River Rivella. Water could then, theoretically, be led down the hillside to feed numerous fountains by gravity flow. Vast quantities of earth were then moved to change the topography of the hill below the monastery so that the garden could be laid out on the same axis as the buildings. Ligorio put his scholarly knowledge of mythological and allegorical references to good effect to create an elaborate checkerboard-pattern garden. The principal public entrance to the garden was through a grove at the base of the hillside, from which was a central axis rising in flights of steps directly to the villa. Off that central axis were cross-axes covered with pergolas that successively screened the next themed phase of the garden, each with terraces of increasing sophistication. To experience those elaborate iconographic sections, visitors needed to walk through the garden. In the next several years when Pope Pius IV and then Pope Gregory XIII did just that during their visits, Cardinal d'Este reputedly attempted to humble them by awaiting them in all his finery at the head of the long climb.

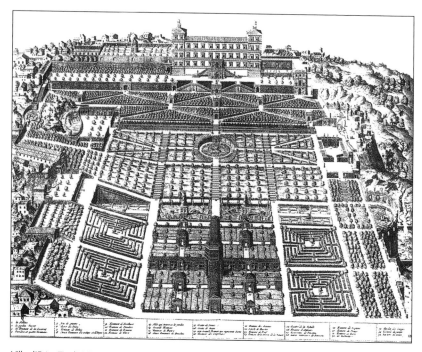

Villa d'Este, Tivoli. Visitors approaching the villa had to pass through several sections of the garden with its impressive water features. (Jellicoe, *The Oxford Companion to Gardens*, Oxford University Press, 1991)

Such contrivances demonstrated man's power over nature in an intriguing, yet amusing, style; and none did this better than fountains. Of the numerous fountains on the various terraces, particularly distinctive was the Fountain of the Owl, the mechanism for which derived from a translation of Heron of Alexandria's *Pneumatica*. A group of bronze automata, it consisted of a flock of birds activated by water pressure singing in a thicket until an owl silently appeared, frightening the birds into silence. When the owl departed the birds would begin to sing again. With the collaboration of Thomaso Chiruchi, an expert on hydraulics, and Claude Venard, a highly regarded Burgundian manufacturer of hydraulic organs, Ligorio also recreated and elaborated another of Heron of Alexandria's ideas – the Fountain of the Water Organ. Then, along one of the side terraces was another elaborate feature – the Avenue of the Hundred Fountains. The wonders of hydraulics had water spurting into a stone trough, from serried rows of moss-covered eagles, lilies and other d'Este motifs. Stone, rather than plants, was used to give the garden colour.

Word of the magnificence of the re-creations of Heron's inventions at Villa d'Este quickly spread. From the reports of visiting ambassadors the fountains came to the attention of European heads of state, who then wanted similar devices for their palace gardens. The band of specialist *fontainieri* Ligorio had convened at Tivoli then moved abroad, most notably to France. Ligorio was himself influential in getting the fountains more widely publicised by replicating them in other Italian villa gardens – at the Villa Lante for example, and even the Casino di Pio IV in Rome – and by his financial patronage of Federico Commandino, who in 1575 published the first full Italian translation of Heron. Then in 1581 a journal was published by Michel de Montaigne giving accounts of how the water organ functioned and showing the close links between Heron's text and the actual fountains at Villa d'Este. Soon many Renaissance gardens contained automata inspired by Heron. The Villa d'Este fountains came to the attention of Salomon de Caus (1572–1626) who diffused knowledge of them further in his work *Les Raison de Forces Mouvantes* (1615). At Wilton House, in Wiltshire, de Caus put some of these devices into effect, most notably the *giochi d'acqua* (water jokes). Concealed jets of water, such as those on the terrace of the Fountain of Venus at Villa d'Este, they could be amusingly switched on to drench

Heron's water organ. (S. Switzer, *An Introduction to a General System of Hydrostaticks and Hydraulicks*, Astley, 1729)

unsuspecting visitors. In 1729 Stephen Switzer popularised some of Heron's more elaborate water engine inventions with his elegantly illustrated book *An Introduction to a General System of Hydrostaticks*. However, a scholarly and accurate translation into English of the *Pneumatica* did not come about until 1851 when the work was edited by Bennet Woodcroft, a senior official (and an accomplished inventor) at the London Patent Office. In Britain knowledge of Heron's ideas that Ligorio had put into effect at the Villa d'Este made sophisticated fountains culturally acceptable and facilitated the efforts of makers of mass-produced fountains – such as the cast-iron monstrosities of the Coalbrookdale Company – in selling their products to the owners of town and suburban gardens.

At Hever Castle, in Kent, one of the most spectacular features was the unique Italian Garden, which contained much statuary and sculpture dating from as long ago as Roman times. These were collected by William Waldorf Astor during his service as American Minister in Rome and brought to Hever Castle between 1903 and 1908. On the south side of the Italian Garden was an immensely long pergola supported by colonnades overhung with branches, all of which sheltered a nearby lengthy three-tiered arrangement of fountains deliberately overgrown with moss. This work was inspired by Ligorio's Avenue of the Hundred Fountains at the Villa d'Este.

Ligorio, who had achieved so much, died in 1583. For a while the Villa d'Este was subject to further improvements, notably with new fountains made by the Renaissance sculptor Giovanni Bernini. The water gardens there became some of the best-known Italian gardens and as a consequence much of the wider world's understanding of Renaissance gardens comes from the Villa d'Este. Even when the grounds fell into disrepair in the eighteenth century Hubert Robert's paintings of the place in a state of ruin helped shape an enduring romantic image of the gardens. During the 1920s the villa and garden, having become the property of the Italian government, were partly restored and opened to the public. Ligorio's masterly creation at Tivoli, so much of which was

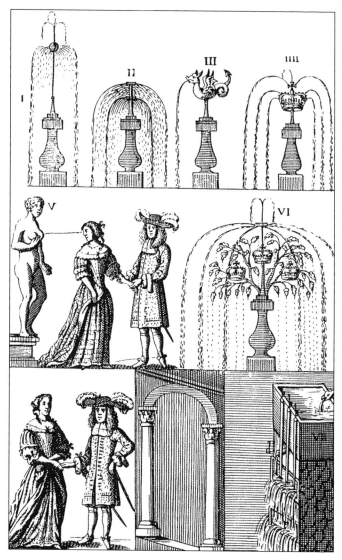

Joke fountains in Italian Renaissance gardens were based on Heron's original designs. (Worlidge, *The Art of Gardening*, 1688)

influenced by the work of Heron, received formal international recognition in 2001 when UNESCO officially listed the Villa d'Este a World Heritage Site.

Villa d'Este, Tivoli, www.villaestetivoli.info; Hever Castle, Kent, www.hevercastle.co.uk; The Fountain Society, www.fountainsoc.org.uk.

Percy Thrower, the Media Presenter

By creating the image of gardening as a popular leisure activity Percy Thrower became a hero who changed people's perceptions of gardening and their gardens. Known at the height of his fame as 'Britain's head gardener', Percy Thrower became involved with broadcasting only by chance.

From his earliest years, Percy's principal ambition had been to follow in his father's horticultural footsteps. Mr Thrower senior was head gardener at Horwood House, a 500-acre Buckinghamshire estate owned by Frederick Denny, an Irish bacon millionaire who had instructed his gardener to develop some 15 acres of fields and woodlands into a magnificent garden. At 14 Percy left school and began working full time at Horwood. The lowliest of the nineteen gardeners on the estate, Percy's first job was in the greenhouses, crocking pots, mixing compost and planting out seedlings. The hours were long: from six thirty in the morning until five thirty in the evening. He augmented his income of a shilling a day by trapping moles and shooting magpies and crows on the estate for sixpence a head. In the four years he worked at

Horwood House, Percy acquitted himself well and assumed he would, like some of his fellow workers, move on to work in the gardens of other country houses. However, he had the good fortune to have a father who knew Charles Cook, the head gardener at Windsor, who agreed to allow Percy to work there. So impressed was Mrs Denny with Percy's appointment at the Royal Gardens that she instructed a chauffeur to take him there in one of the Horwood House cars.

At Windsor, Percy was one of sixty gardeners working in a disciplined hierarchy as strict as a ship's company. Percy became one of twenty 'improvers' and spent his first two years in the fruit department. According to Shirley Du Boulay's historical work *The Gardeners*, such was Percy's rapid progress that eventually he came to be in charge of the flower decoration of the Royal Enclosure at Ascot. Four years later, Thrower left the Royal Gardens to move to his first position in amenity horticulture, taking on a post with the City of Leeds Parks Department as a journeyman-gardener. Common practice for ambitious trainee gardeners was to move from place to place building up experience; and after two years at Leeds, he moved again, this time to Derby Parks Department. Some weeks after the outbreak of the Second World War he married Connie Cook, a daughter of the Windsor head gardener, in Sandringham Church. During the war he continued with the Derby Parks Department, growing produce in the Dig for Victory campaign. Then in 1946 he was appointed parks superintendent at Shrewsbury, and his name became synonymous with the town's fine gardening tradition. He was responsible for rejuvenating the Shrewsbury Flower Show, one of the country's principal horticultural shows.

One morning in autumn 1948 Thrower was working in his office when the BBC presenter Godfrey Baseley walked in and

The first celebrity television horticulturist, Percy Thrower (1913–88), who became known as 'Britain's Head Gardener'. (IPC/*Amateur Gardening*)

invited him to appear for ten minutes on a radio programme about gardening in Shrewsbury. The request changed Thrower's life. He immediately proved himself to be such a natural on radio that the BBC retained him until 1951 to present the show (which became known as *In Your Garden*), consisting of a series of broadcasts from other people's gardens. Clearly he had a flair for the electronic media and a gift for putting over very simply any gardening subject. To his credit, although he had worked in the Royal Gardens he was never condescending. His quiet, friendly voice with his countryman's accent and his relaxed style were evidently endearing to the public. He tended to work without a script, believing that if a presenter knew his subject the plant should form enough of an inspiration for the words to appear. So when in 1956 the BBC began doing a monthly television series on horticulture, *Gardening Club*, Thrower was also persuaded to present that – and the show's viewing figure rose to some 5 million viewers week by week. The programme was filmed entirely in a studio, and in order to hear Percy properly microphones were concealed in soil. Another innovation was to have a greenhouse – albeit without any glass – in the studio. To show viewers he was purposeful and informal, his trademark gimmick whenever he walked into his greenhouse in the studio would be to take off his jacket and hang it on a nail.

When colour television arrived in 1969 *Gardening Club* evolved into *Gardener's World*, with Thrower as the main presenter. He was by now regarded as 'Britain's head gardener'. Many of the TV broadcasts were made outside his own home near Shrewsbury, a simple modern four-bedroomed bungalow called 'The Magnolias', with a few acres of garden. Significantly, in the process of making practical horticulture more comprehensible to the general public, Percy was knowingly sacrificing his own privacy by letting the TV cameras in. Sometimes the television do-it-yourself expert Barry Bucknell would appear on screen giving advice to viewers on simple garden construction projects. 'The Magnolias' became a household name – some 5,000 people turned up one weekend when the grounds were opened for charity – and its association with painting and DIY seems to have been a cause of the remarkable success of magnolia-colour paint. Thrower worked the garden himself and seemed quite unfussed when, almost every week, a forty-strong TV crew arrived to film the next programme.

All those television appearances enabled him to communicate his knowledge, enjoyment and understanding of gardening to the wider British public. Additionally, he helped to promote gardening by other means, lecturing widely throughout the country and taking part in the radio programmes *The Brains' Trust* and *Gardeners' Question Time*. He acquired such an enormous public popularity that platform appearances around the land invariably attracted large audiences. He became the prototype of all TV gardeners, seeming in public to project a sense of quiet reassurance such as a Harley Street specialist would envy. Without a script he relied on his own good research of a subject, which helped overcome the tension he felt before going on air.

Curiously, Percy Thrower never had a contract with the BBC, working for them only on an ad hoc basis. However, in 1976 he was abruptly dropped by the programme because he breached the BBC's 'No advertising policy' by agreeing to figure in a series of ICI Garden Plus fertiliser commercials on ITV. Newspaper headlines appeared such as 'Percy Throw-out', 'Mr Greenfingers Pruned by BBC'. The BBC contended he could not profess to offer impartial advice when linked with a particular firm. Thrower was deeply upset by the programme's decision. However, his sense of obligation to inform the public on gardening was undaunted. He switched his attentions to Independent television. Also, when the opportunity arose to be the gardening presenter on BBC TV's

The Magnolias: Thrower's own house and gardens from where he produced hundreds of TV broadcasts. By making his home a household name, Thrower inadvertently increased the popularity of magnolia paint! (IPC/*Amateur Gardening*)

children's programme *Blue Peter* he readily agreed. Operating from a patch of garden only a few yards square he created at the BBC's Television Centre, he appeared many times on *Blue Peter* over a period of nearly fourteen years, during which time he provided millions of children with their first instruction to basic gardening techniques. Despite his rather grandfatherly persona, he was just as successful at talking about gardening to children as he had been when broadcasting to adults.

Being a famous TV horticulturalist he achieved the curious distinction of being the first gardener to appear in wax at Madame Tussauds! Regardless of his celebrity status – he even appeared on the *Morecombe and Wise Show* and starred on *This is Your Life* – he kept his feet on the ground and continued to work at Shrewsbury until his retirement in 1974. He also exercised his entrepreneurial skill. In 1967 he was asked to advise on the setting up of a garden centre at Syon Park, and became a director of the initial enterprise. Believing it to have been overcomplicated he pondered starting his own business, and in 1970 was able to put that ambition into effect when he acquired an existing 40-acre rose nursery from Murrells near Shrewsbury and converted it into Percy Thrower's Gardening Centre. Fame did not isolate him from the public. He liked nothing better than to puff away on his pipe behind the counter at his garden centre, or on some horticultural stand at the Chelsea Flower Show, dispensing advice to anyone who had a few questions.

Among the other promotional ventures he was involved with there was a travel firm which he partly owned. It arranged for him personally to take parties of amateur gardeners on luxury cruises to visit some of the world's most notable maritime gardens, and even chartered a Dakota aircraft to fly such enthusiasts to see the Dutch bulb fields. He also wrote a weekly column on

Edward Stewart's Garden Centre

Britain's first supermarket-style garden centre appeared at Ferndown, near Bournemouth, in 1953. Its founder was Edward Stewart, a member of the Scottish dynasty of foresters and nurserymen who had originally gone into business in Dundee in the eighteenth century. Their Dorset branch, at Ferndown, had been established as long ago as 1859; and it was by adapting the existing sheds there that Edward Stewart opened the centre, which would eventually become known as 'Stewart's Gardenlands'. Other nursery owners, having visited the United States and seen how sales of plants in simple containers – even in old jam tins – could make garden centres viable, returned home and started their own. Such were Notcutts, at Woodbridge in 1958, Wyevale, at Hereford in 1961, then Pennells, at Lincoln in 1966. Their high-profile growth overshadowed the ingenuity of Edward Stewart's pioneering innovation.

current work in *Amateur Gardening*. His many books include *In the Flower Garden*, *In Your Garden* and *Colour in Your Garden*. Percy Thrower's contribution to horticulture was honoured by an MBE, and also a medal from the RHS. At the time of his death in 1988 he was still getting as much enjoyment from judging simple county flower shows as he had when appearing as the nation's favourite gardening presenter. Thrower's real accomplishment, however, was that he introduced the country to gardening by simply caring for plants.

Horwood House, Bucks, www.iaccuk.org; Percy Thrower's
Gardening and Leisure, www.shropshiretourism.infon;
Shrewsbury Flower Show, www.shrewsburyflowershow.org.uk.

Thomas Church's Timber Decking

The controversial craze for garden decking, in the last few years,
has been attributed to the influence of television gardening
makeover programmes. In fact, the phenomenon was begun
several decades ago in the United States by the celebrated designer
Thomas Church. Although his distinctive work established new
ingenious garden design features to cope with the needs of
modern life, his gardens, many of which were designed for private
clients, have since not been easy to visit.

Born in Boston in 1902, Thomas Dolville Church was taken as
an infant by his mother to Southern California, growing up near
Los Angeles. Abandoning an early ambition to be a lawyer, he
studied garden design at the University of California, Berkeley,
graduating in 1922, then at Harvard's Graduate School of Design,
where he enrolled for a Masters degree course in landscape
architecture. In 1927, having obtained a Sheldon Travelling
Fellowship, he went on a European tour to research his MA thesis
on the influence of Italian architecture on American gardens.
Visiting Spain and Italy, the newly married Church took photos of
formal gardens such as the Generalife and overgrown Villa d'Este;
then, when he returned home, he also visited some recently built
gardens in California.

Already perceiving there to be a lack of correlation in Californian gardens and houses, and having an eye to a future career, Thomas Church entitled his completed dissertation: 'A study of Mediterranean gardens and their adaptability to California conditions'. Prophetically, in the report of his Grand Tour, he wrote: 'California is developing a style of its own, suited to its needs and fitting into its hillsides as naturally as the Generalife among its olive groves.' The Depression was in full swing in 1930 when Church, after a spell teaching construction techniques at Ohio State University, began his own garden design business, opening a small office at Pasatiempo, near San Cruz, California. Jobs were scarce so at that time he was fortunate to obtain work as a resident architect (an 'improver' at a golfing complex housing project near Pasatiempo), tending existing gardens and selecting sites. At Berkeley and Harvard he had been steeped in the conventional *beaux-arts* tradition of formality in the gardens of grand Mediterranean houses, so, naturally, Church at that stage in his career sought to apply some elements of that elegance in his early designs.

A particularly significant attempt to do so was at the so-called Butler House designed by William Wurster, a modern architect specialising in timber houses. Church created an airy courtyard whose centrepiece was an old Californian oak tree, which he meticulously trimmed himself to show a sculptural shape. From that time on the careful clipping of existing Californian oak trees would become one of several Thomas Church trademarks. Later, in his definitive book *Gardens Are for People* (1955) Church would advise owners to: 'Look carefully at your trees to be sure you have developed all they have to give you. Their beauty is not in foliage alone but in their shape and branching and in the relation of their structure to their foliage.'

Thomas Church (1902–78), the populariser of garden deckscaping. (Environment Design Archives, Berkeley, California)

Church had realised by then that the steep-sided hills of San Francisco necessitated specialist forms of gardens. The demands of new urban life meant the increasing use of garden space by families living in smaller houses, and the need for low-maintenance gardens. Clearly what was required was a new form of garden design. Remembering the art deco exhibition of French design and abstract cubist painters he had seen while in Paris in 1927, Church now wondered if cubism could be applied to garden design. In 1937 he made his second visit to Europe, to Scandinavia, where in Finland he met Alvar and Aino Aalto, whose free-flowing architecture inspired him to adopt more relaxed, informal and organic garden plans. Already, Church was going over to an almost wholly abstract style in his garden designs and had begun to experiment with angular forms that gave the illusion of greater size – the most innovative and widely known example being the Sullivan Garden in 1937, where the longer arm of an L-shaped zigzag path covered two-thirds of the diagonal of a rectangular site. It was remarkable for its use of bold cubist diagonal geometry which created a lively sense of perspective as it cut across the site. As Michael Laurie noted in *An Introduction to Landscape Architecture*: 'Church developed a theory based on cubism, that a garden should have no beginning and no end and that it should be pleasing when seen from any angle, not only from the house.'

Church's new approach was first realised in two garden designs for the Golden Gate Exposition in 1939. The central axis was finally abandoned in favour of a multiplicity of viewpoints and the use of asymmetrical lines to create an apparent increase in the dimensions of the site. In a study sketch that he presented for one of the designs, a lawned area is clearly surrounded by horizontal timber decking, thereby making it the first Church design to advocate decking.

Timber planking was widely used in Thomas Church's own house and garden. (By permission of Megan Toms and *The Mediterranean Garden*)

Church's emphasis on flooring as an essential part of a garden's composition became most famously apparent in 1947 with a pool garden he began designing for the wealthy Donnell family (owners of Marathon Oil of Ohio), who had recently acquired a 4,000-acre ranch in California's undeveloped Sonoma valley. Church drew his inspiration from the breathtakingly picturesque setting, a surrounding countryside of gentle hills, salt marshes with sinuous channels and a scattering of live oaks. Accordingly, he made the garden's central feature – a ground-level swimming pool – into a curvaceous kidney shape with its own abstract sculpted island. Surrounding the pool was an audaciously linear-effect terrace of sharp square concrete slabs, beyond which, to extend the area of activity, was redwood decking carefully cut in a pattern of squares to allow space for the live oaks. Almost as soon as the El Novillero pool terrace had been completed in 1948 photos of it were featured in many magazines, and then books, in the United States, Canada and Europe (continuing to the present). Influentially hailed in 1953 as a twentieth-century garden design classic, Church's Donnell garden became the prototype for a generation of modern landscape architectural gardens, including roof gardens.

The Donnell garden established Church's name. Yet while his assistants, such as Lawrence Halprin and others who had worked with him at El Novillero, went on to design grand public works projects, Church, despite his genius, commendably remained committed to designing small private gardens. Shrewdly he extended the recognition of his name by means of writing. In the 1930s he had begun writing articles for a publication called *Sunset*. Subtitled the 'Magazine for Western Living', it was the creation of the Southern Pacific Railroad, owners of large tracts of the west which they wanted to prepare for settlement.

Church quickly established a personal writing style: typically his sentences were short, his mood sparkling and at times whimsical, at times just practical. Extraordinarily prolific, Church also began writing for the then East Coast *House & Garden* and several popular architectural magazines, such as *California Arts and Architecture*. In a series of articles for the latter on the subject of the small Californian garden he claimed: 'The small garden is like a small room. It must be neat . . . Doors are replacing windows . . . Dining rooms open to paved courts . . . Everything points to the increasing intimacy of the house and its garden.' This, Church pointed out – bridging practicality with august learning – was not a new idea: the Egyptians, Greeks, Romans and the Renaissance Italians had all integrated their houses and gardens, and lived out of doors.

The publication that more than any other enabled Church to enjoy a remarkably high level of visibility and national reputation was the New York-based *House Beautiful*, for whose Editor-in-Chief, Elizabeth Gordon, he designed a garden in 1946 and with whom he forged a lasting friendship. From that year until her retirement in 1965, his work appeared regularly in *House Beautiful*. Because the magazine's brand of modernism emphasised the importance of indoor and outdoor connections, Church's garden designs often appeared just right. None of his North American contemporaries were lionised by the press to the extent that Church was. His relationship with *House Beautiful* was unprecedented and a subject of genuine envy among other garden designers. It was *House Beautiful* that in April 1951 famously showed the Donnell pool garden on its cover, which was to make that garden a design classic.

Church's hitherto most innovative use of decking had been at Aptos on the Californian coast, where in 1938 William Wurster had constructed a timber beach house for the Martin family.

The Martin Garden, at Aptos – a distinctive Thomas Church design advertised in 1956 by the California Redwood Association to encourage householders to build garden decking. (*House & Home*, 1956)

THOMAS D. CHURCH, leading landscape architect for over twenty years, has done outstanding work for private estates and subdivisions, hotels and schools, industrial plants and government agencies, both here and abroad Well known for his articles in *House Beautiful*, he is also the author of the new best-selling book, *Gardens are for People*.

Of Garden Redwood, Mr. Church says…"Used alone or in com bination with other materials, redwood is one of my most versatile materials. By specifying the correct grade of CRA redwood, I can obtain the effect I want, every time."

Gardens are for people . . . just as houses are…and they should receive the same careful planning and material specifications as architectural structures. For design ideas, construction details, and data on Garden Redwood grades, write on your letterhead for our Landscape Architect's File.

California Redwood

CALIFORNIA REDWOOD ASSOCIATION
576 SACRAMENTO STREET
SAN FRANCISCO 11, CALIFORNIA

There, in 1946, having been called upon to landscape the garden, Church opted to do only some simple planting, yet created a shapely curved central sandy area to occupy a position conventionally taken by a lawn or pool. The boundary he created between the house and sand was formed by a deck of redwood planks set in a large parquet flooring-type pattern with a zigzag edge. Integrated into this were built-in benches (which would be commonplace in gardens later in the twentieth century). Particularly keen to capitalise on the beautiful use of such flooring were the California Redwood Association, who in April 1956 ran a full-page illustrated advertisement in *House & Home* extolling the virtues of timber decking. The association used a testimonial quote from Church in the advertisement to show how a perfect garden might be instantly achieved by using the decking: 'I can', said Church, 'obtain the effect I want every time.'

In 1955 Church further extolled the practical advantages of decking in a section of his first book, *Gardens Are for People*: 'For the home owner on a budget – and name one who isn't – a deck can serve as the ideal compromise, using natural materials in an outdoor setting but retaining the low-maintenance attractions of a practical space paved in concrete.' Many years later environmentalists criticised the use of wooden flooring in gardens for blocking rainwater from the ground and being a wasteful use of timber. Thus it was ironic that in *Gardens Are for People* Church had condemned as inexcusable those who carelessly damaged trees by concreting underneath them: 'Drainage and aeration may prevent such a calamity, but why take a chance when decks offer a safe alternative?' In fact he insisted that, if done properly, decking made 'it possible to enjoy a close relationship with the native oaks at the floor level of the house. And, most important, the lives of the trees are not endangered.'

Decking, outdoors lighting and railway sleepers, such as in this Californian plot designed by Church before his death in 1978 became commonplace features in British gardens several years later. (Huxley, *An Illustrated History of Gardening*, Paddington Press, 1978)

Church's advice to gardeners in 1955 to use decking was repeated in numerous high-profile magazine articles and was then reinforced in his second and final book *Your Private World* (1969). By the time of his death in August 1978 Church was variously estimated to have designed between 1,500 and 4,000 gardens in North America. Socially prestigious though ownership of a 'Tommy Church' garden was, and increasingly became, his gardens began to acquire a reputation for falling apart, mostly in terms of cracks appearing in the unreinforced paving and simple asphalt he had used. The Redwood decking seems to have endured best. In Britain the idea of timber decking was initially imported by John Brookes, whose 1969 book *Room Outside* had pictures of Church-influenced gardens. Brookes's idea much shaped the thinking of a rising band of young British designers, such as Alan Titchmarsh and Diarmuid Gavin, whose extensive use of decking in garden makeover TV programmes was readily acknowledged to be workable by viewers whose growing experience of Mediterranean holidays had given them an appetite for outdoors living in their own gardens. Thomas Church was the real hero, or some might think villain, of British garden decking, even though he himself had been inspired by the European gardens he had visited on his initial Grand Tour of Europe as long ago as the 1920s.

Denmans, John Brookes's horticultural school near Arundel in Sussex, has examples of early British decking.

Caius Martius's Ornate Hedging

An especially love-it-or-loathe-it garden feature is topiary. Throughout Britain garden centres are increasingly selling topiaried shrubs, whose apparently Mediterranean characteristics make it natural to assume that they originated in Renaissance times. In fact, the person whom gardeners really have to thank for originating the skill of topiary lived many centuries earlier.

The real populariser of topiary was a Roman born in 38 BC named Caius Martius (sometimes known as Matius Calvena). Although it is believed that he also invented various techniques of horticultural propagation, Martius was by no means a professional gardener. He was better known as a writer of popular comedies, and quite why he should have advocated the trimming of hedges into whimsical shapes is unclear. However, politics and artistic influence were closely allied in Imperial Rome, and it was possibly Caesar Augustus's patronage of Martius's inventions that led to topiary being emulated by the Roman nobility. It was they who began using topiary to enliven the forecourts of their houses, which hitherto had been quite plain.

The epigram writer Martial, and then Pliny the Elder, were sure it was Caius Martius who introduced the first topiary to Roman gardens. In *Historia Naturalis* (AD 70) Pliny revealed how the ancient Mediterranean cypress (*Cupressus sempervirens*) was increasingly being planted not only to form screens in vineyards, 'but nowadays is clipped or rounded off to a slender outline, and even used in the landscape gardener's art to make representations of hunting scenes, fleets of ships and imitations of real objects'. In approximately AD 100 more detailed descriptions of Roman gardens with topiary were made in letters written by Pliny the Younger (the nephew of Pliny the Elder). In these letters he describes the gardens of his own villa in the foothills of the Apennines in Tuscany as being:

> embellished by various figures, and grounded with a box hedge, from which you descend by an easy slope, adorned with the representation of divers animals in box. This is surrounded by a walk enclosed with evergreens shaped into a variety of forms. Behind it is the Gestatio laid out in the form of a circus, ornamental in the middle with box, cut into numberless different figures, together with a plantation of shrubs prevented by the shears from running to high. The whole is fenced in by a wall, covered with box, rising in differing ranges to the top.

The physical act of gardening in those times was done only by slaves, each of whom was assigned a specific responsibility. Indeed, the word 'topiary' developed from the slaves in charge of the ornamental garden (*topia*), who were known as *topiaries*. So it was that Pliny the Younger (AD 62–110) observed: 'the box is cut into a thousand different forms, sometimes into letters expressing the name of the master, sometimes that of the artificer, whilst here and there little obelisks rise intermixed alternately with fruit trees'. That Roman gardens should have had the name of the slave spelt out in topiary lettering shows how highly regarded as a specialist art form topiary had already become.

In just a few decades the fashion for topiary spread throughout much of the Roman Empire. It apparently reached Britain sometime after AD 43 where for the next 400 years it was grown within the confines of Roman residences. Archaeological evidence of early such topiary has been found at Fishbourne, in Sussex, on the site of a ruined palace which surrounded a rectangular

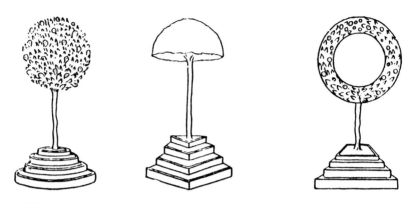

In 1467 the *Hypnerotomachia* showed the first-ever prints of the topiary Martius had pioneered. (Clevely, *Topiary: The Art of Clipping*, Salem House, 1988)

garden that included a wide walk enclosed by other smaller paths. Along the sides of each of these have been found narrow trenches of rich soil, almost certainly dug out to provide cultivated beds for ornamental hedges that would probably have been made of clipped box (much in the style popular in later centuries for edging kitchen garden beds). According to A.M. Clevely's historical work *Topiary*, even more specific archaeological evidence has been found at Frocester, in Gloucestershire, where excavation of a fourth-century villa garden has revealed trenches dug for hedges beside paths, this time together with charcoal positively identified as having come from box shrubs.

While Martius has been credited as the creator of topiary, in recent years archaeological evidence in the form of ancient pictures has raised the possibility that the origins of topiary might be earlier still. The slaves of the imperial city of Rome would have been Greek, Syrian or Egyptian and might have introduced topiary from other lands – perhaps from Persia where the army of Alexander the Great had found hedges of clipped myrtle.

During Martius's time, and for centuries afterwards, ornamental bushes had been trimmed with sharp pruning knives and sprung clippers (invented by the Romans for the purpose of sheep shearing and referred to by Pliny the Younger as 'shears'). Martius's topiary invention seems to have vanished from Britain when the Romans left, although when the empire became centred on Constantinople, that style of gardening reached a fantastical stage, whereby topiary itself was replaced by exotically jewelled trees, which were often further decorated with colourful birds. But during the Dark Ages topiary effectively disappeared from all gardens in Europe, until the Renaissance when it re-emerged in even more extravagant forms.

The person most influential in reviving Martius's invention was Leone Battista Alberti, a versatile Renaissance character who, in addition to his accomplishments as a painter, sculptor and socialite at the papal court, was an outstandingly brilliant architect. He was one of the earliest architects to argue for the correct use of the classical orders and, reputedly, his *De re aedificatoria* (1450) was the first printed book on architecture. The section on gardening in that book was much influenced by the writings of Pliny the Elder, whose ideas on topiary Alberti put into practical effect at Villa Quaracchi, a villa he designed to be built in Florence in 1449. The topiary there figured prominently in the forms of spheres, porticoes, temples, vases, urns, apes, donkeys, oxen, giants, witches, philosophers and even cardinals and popes! Alberti was not long alone in his enthusiasm for topiary: in 1467 the monk Francesco Colonna, using the pseudonym of Polyphilius, published a long allegorical story, *Hypnerotomachia*, recounting a vision in which many scenes were enacted in imaginary gardens. Within these were clipped hedges of myrtle and cypress, hyssop trimmed into spheres and shaped junipers in

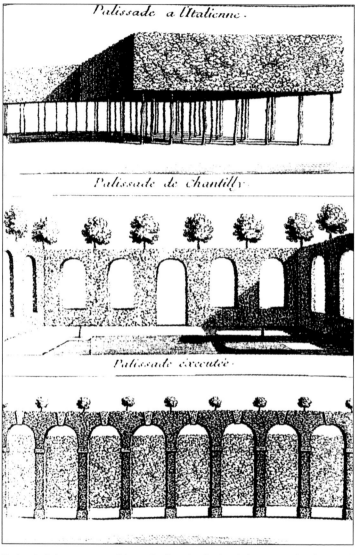

Topiary techniques were used to create elegant palisades. (John James, *The Theory and Practice of Gardening*, James, 1712)

large pots. Containing pictures of topiary never seen before, the *Hypnerotomachia* proved to be an enduring influence on subsequent Italian garden design. Colonna's ideas were disseminated by being borrowed by other writers such as François Rabelais and even William Shakespeare.

Thus began what was to be the Golden Age of Topiary in Europe and most notably in France, where by 1520 terrace beds in the garden at the castle of Gaillon, near Rouen, were being formally edged with hedges probably of scented herbs or box. The level beds there were arranged in a series of small square patterns or knots, each enclosed by dwarf hedging which was also used to construct low mazes. This literally set the pattern for later French parterres, which increasingly consisted of interwoven clipped box hedges. Nowhere were such parterres more extensively employed than at Versailles, which Louis XIV developed to visually demonstrate the strength of the monarchy's power to dominate France and, by implication, its natural landscape. To create that effect, André Le Notre, who was responsible for implementing the overall grand design at Versailles, brought in some 30,000 labourers to reshape the grounds. Between 1662 and 1699 Le Notre planted out palisades and outdoor rooms, and also stately avenues that accorded with points of the compass. Although the topiary at Versailles was undertaken on an epic scale, with obelisks at the corners of parterre gardens and potted trees trimmed as spheres on standards, it was still less complicated than the style of earlier Italian gardens.

Le Notre's respect for topiary was introduced to England by one of his principal disciples, Guillaume Beaumont, who between 1689 and 1712 worked in Cumbria improving the garden at Levens Hall. There Beaumont planted beech and yew hedges to divide the garden into distinctive compartments. On the parterre

Levens Hall led the revival of topiary in Britain. In response to the advocates of the landscape style of garden, elaborate topiary gardens had become an increasingly rare sight. (Blomfield and Thomas, *The Formal Garden in England*, Macmillan, 1892)

he began topiaring what was to become a magnificent collection of yews. At Levens Hall, and elsewhere in the country, topiary was surprisingly *less* constrained than in France. Indeed, as the craze for topiary grew throughout England, almost any garden plant – including holly, privet and even rosemary – was vulnerable to being clipped into a fancy shape regardless of its suitability.

Fun though Martius's topiary invention was, it would soon be virtually swept from England by a change in the tide of garden fashion. Topiary fell in the frontline of attack on the artificiality of formal gardens, and especially those that were perceived to be French in style. In an influential article that appeared in the *Spectator* in 1712, the politician Joseph Addison devastatingly wrote:

Our British gardeners on the contrary, instead of humouring Nature, love to deviate from it as much as possible. Our trees rise in cones, globes and pyramids. We see the mark of the scissors on every plant and bush. I do not know whether I am singular in my opinion, but for my part, I would rather look upon a tree in all its luxuriancy and diffusion of boughs and branches, than when it is thus cut and trimmed into a mathematical figure.

The death knell came in 1713 in the form of the 'Verdant Sculpture', a famously satirical piece by Alexander Pope in the *Guardian*, in which he mockingly described topiary as, 'Adam and Eve in yew; Adam a little shattered by the fall of the tree of knowledge in the great storm; Eve and the serpent very flourishing. The tower of Babel, not yet finished.'

Such grew to be the popularity of the landscape movement, that by the mid-eighteenth century most of England's formal gardens were grubbed up and replaced with 'natural'-looking landscapes. Topiaries were simply removed or allowed to grow out to their natural forms. Thenceforth, until at least the early twentieth century, they continued to be perceived as being in poor taste. But there were a few notable exceptions: Levens Hall, in Cumbria; Packwood House, Warwickshire; and the contoured hedges of

Powis Castle, Powys. So geographically remote were these locations that their topiary could remain intact regardless of what was considered stylish in the rest of the country. The only other examples to exist were individual pieces in workers' cottage gardens – a proletarian element that only worsened its then somewhat artless image.

The glimmerings of revival started with the advocacy of traditionally formal aesthetics in John Sedding's *Garden Craft Old and New* (1891), then Reginald Blomfield's *The Formal Garden in England* (1892). Early demand was perceived in the form of an increase in business for William Cutbush, a Highgate nurseryman who had begun importing ornately clipped shrubs from the Netherlands. The Dutch were old masters of topiary and supplied the English market. Cutbush acquired his from the Boskoop district of the Netherlands, as well as growing and training many thousands of

Details of topiary techniques that might have been practised in Martius's time were explained to British readers by Nathaniel Lloyd in 1925. (Lloyd, *Garden Craftsmanship in Yew and Box*, Ernest Benn, 1925)

topiary shrubs in his own nursery. The strengthening of interest
Cutbush had detected was accelerated in 1925 by the publication
of *Garden Craftsmanship in Yew and Box* by Nathaniel Lloyd. An
architectural historian who in 1910 enlarged Great Dixter, his
own fine garden in East Sussex, Lloyd drew on his experiences
there to show how topiary shrubs ought best be grown. By then
appeared also some elegantly sturdy new topiary growths at
Nymans, in West Sussex (1890), Compton Wynyates, Warwickshire (1895), and Hidcote, Gloucestershire (1908).

Belatedly, better tools to cope with the maintenance of such
bushes were by then becoming available. Charles Estienne's
Maison Rustique, translated as *The Countrey Farme* in 1616,
advised that topiary should be trimmed with something 'like those
which tailors use' – wooden-handled shears (which are now a

Ingenious tools were created in the nineteenth
century for hedge trimming, and Ridgway's multi-
headed clippers are seen here. (Beeton, *The Book
of Garden Management*, Ward Lock, 1872)

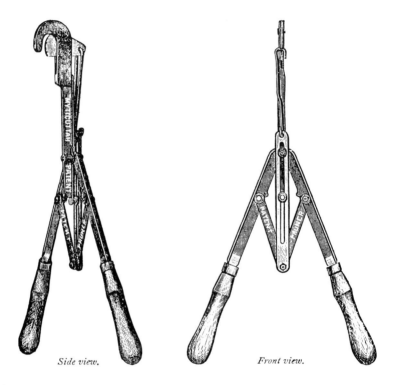

Side view.   *Front view.*

The 'Myticuttah' used on inaccessible parts of hedges. (James Brown, *The Forester*, Blackwood, 1894)

familiar sight in most gardens). The especially significant evolutionary advancement on that commonplace device appeared in Britain during the late nineteenth century in the form of shears with fearsome multiple blades (perhaps as many as ten), some models of which were even set in a semicircular pattern. The reciprocating multi-cutter principle was also used on the lengthy cutting bars of horse-drawn agricultural mowing clippers. In the late 1920s these design ideas were combined to create the 'Little Wonder', a British hedge trimmer powered by a hand wheel, rather like that of an eggwhisk! Very soon afterwards an improved model became available enabling even amateur gardeners to do their topiary with hand-held 'Little Wonder' clippers powered by a simple electric motor.

Some of the finest topiary in Britain is at Levens Hall, Cumbria, www.levenshall.co.uk; and the late Christopher Lloyd's Great Dixter Gardens, East Sussex, www.greatdixter.co.uk.

Worst Devices for Accidents

Devices	Accidents Per Year (UK average)
Lawnmowers	6,500
Flowerpots	5,300
Secateurs and pruners	4,400
Spades	3,600
Hedge trimmers	3,100

(Royal Society for the Prevention of Accidents, 2004)

2

Garden Spoilers

Advertisements from the *Gardeners' Chronicle*. (*Gardeners' Chronicle*, 29 August 1953 (above) and 31 October 1953 (left))

Charles Isham's Gnomes

Love them or loath them, gnomes provoke enormous passion in gardens. They have the remarkable capacity to be simultaneously adored by their enthusiasts, yet perceived as irritating frivolities by those who reckon them to be villains. Surprisingly, the innovator who introduced gnomes into Britain was a well-meaning aristocrat.

It all started at Lamport Hall, a fine Northamptonshire country house that had been the home of the Isham family since 1560. John Isham, a successful wool merchant and man of learning, built a new manor house there in 1568 and unwittingly established a family tradition of property improvements. In 1655 the Ishams had the gardens laid out by Gilbert Clarke and the house extended by Inigo Jones's son-in-law, John Webb – making it one of the earliest residences in England to be remodelled in the Inigo Jones style. Additional wings were added and further work on the garden was begun in 1819 by Mary Close, a redoubtable Irish lady who was wife of the eighth baronet. As a consequence of the suicide of her eldest son, in 1846 Charles Isham succeeded to the baronetcy.

Then aged 27, Sir Charles Isham, the tenth baronet, initially concerned himself with *noblesse oblige* duties, becoming sheriff for Northamptonshire. Not much enjoying public office – or even hunting with the Spencers, his neighbours at Althorp – he soon retreated to the confines of the family estate at Lamport Hall, where he carried out a number of improvements, most notably rebuilding cottages in the village in a decorative style. Having inherited his mother's love of gardening, it became a subject on which he concentrated much of his energy. Surrounded by a spacious park planted with sycamores and cedars, the Lamport gardens were tranquil, partly enclosed by Clarke's seventeenth-century banks. In 1847 Charles embarked on an ambitious project, the building of a huge crescent-shaped rockery alongside the house. Isham constructed, reputedly with his own hands, a 24ft-high craggy wall of local ironstone. From the lawns the wall looked as though it was a ruined remnant of a previous mansion, but behind it was the cascade of the alpine garden, falling into a deep dell. Measuring 90ft long, the rockery was reputedly one of the largest examples of the period and one of the earliest in England. It was deliberately placed to face north to allow the plants the greatest chance of flowering in the mild climate. Isham planted it with a variety of alpines and miniature trees, many of some rarity. In 1903 the *Northampton Herald* claimed the only other rockery comparable with it had been constructed by the Emperor of Austria's gardener in Austria.

Having married in 1847 Emily Vaughan, the daughter of a distinguished magistrate, and then produced three children, Charles Isham seemed quite settled. But, inexplicably, he soon left the running of the estate to his capable wife, and retreated into a fantasy world. He developed a fondness for vegetarianism and a talent for writing quite appalling poetry, such as: 'The Lamport fête of '88 I never shall forget, They danced with umbrella up by reason of the wet.' Significantly, his other main enthusiasm was spiritualism.

A system of mystical communication with the unseen world, spiritualism was at that time hardly heard of in Britain. Nor was it

Sir Charles Isham, the aristocratic villain who imported gnomes. (Lamport Hall Preservation Trust)

to be until 1926 when the high-profile believer – Sir Arthur Conan Doyle – popularised it with his book *The History of Spiritualism*. However, spiritualism had long been part of cultural life in Germany and other countries in northern Europe, and sometimes manifested itself in the form of veneration of gnomes. The term 'gnome' had been coined in the sixteenth century in Paracelsus's *Occulta Philosophia*, which categorised each of the four elements as having its own indigenous quasi-spiritual being: sylphs (air), nymphs (water), salamanders (fire), and gnomes (who were responsible for geological activity). A claim that some Germans believed in the existence of dwarfs who lived in caves had reached England in 1730 via Georg Behrens's *The Natural History of the Hartz-Forest in King George's German Dominions*. This book snootily referred to 'Dwarf-holes' between Elbingerode and Rubeland that 'The Common People are positive that were inhabited by Dwarfs'. Reportedly the first gnome specifically intended for use in a garden was made of terracotta and went on sale in Thuringia, Germany, in the 1800s.

In 1847 Sir Charles Isham became the first garden owner to introduce gnomes into Britain. He imported several porcelain dwarf-like figures from Nuremberg, initially with the idea of using them to hold place names at the table. Reputedly it was sometime between 1850 and 1859 that he decided to populate Lamport Hall's rockery with a workforce of gnomes. Perhaps he was inspired by a personal visit he is said to have made to Nuremberg. In any event the hand-modelled gnomes arrived from Germany and Isham busily arranged them in the rockery, giving them spades and pick axes to wield and wheelbarrows to push, as though they were mining. For those who worked at various coal, crystal and diamond mines he made banners protesting that they were 'On Strike'. He personally attended to the rockery on a daily basis, and built a wing of the house, which contained his bedroom, to overlook the site and enable him to keep a watchful eye on his gnomes who, to him, were real people.

When the Ishams held fêtes at Lamport for local charities, Sir Charles wrote and privately printed two explanatory booklets, *Lamport Rockery* and *Notes on Gnomes*. The first written revelation to the world beyond Lamport of the existence of the Isham gnomes' enclave appeared in September 1859 in the form of an article in the *Cottage Gardener*. The next recorded writing, by Isham himself, was 'Visions of fairy blacksmiths at Work', an illustrated article for the spiritualist journal *Medium and Daybreak* in November 1889. Here he extolled the virtues of gnomes, especially because – so he claimed – mines were inhabited by races of such beings who by their lights and knockings led miners to the best seams of the various minerals to be found! In 1897 the *Gardener's Chronicle* published plans of the rockery and photographs of the gnomes at Lamport. Isham himself, although he wrote in favour of gnomes, never seems to have deliberately recommended that other people use them in gardens.

The existence of the Isham gnomes was revealed to the outside world by this picture in the *Gardeners' Chronicle* in the 1890s. (Bedfordshire and Luton Archives Service)

In fact, during the early decades of the gnomes' appearance in Britain, the little bearded wonders were almost entirely promoted by commercial interests, chiefly by the German manufacturer August Heissner. In 1872 Heissner effectively invented the ceramic garden gnome-making industry by founding a factory in Thuringia which turned them out from moulds and hand painted them. Several other gnome businesses sprang up around the town, making Thuringia the gnome capital of Europe. In October 1908 the *Connoisseur* magazine ran the first English advertisement for garden gnomes. The prestigious ceramics firm of Ernest Wahliss was claiming: 'One of our clients has over one hundred of these gnomes in his famous subterranean passages and gardens.' The client was Sir Frank Crisp of Friar Park, whose gnomes were described in his Guide Book for 1906.

Absurd though gnomes were, the actual concept of annotating gardens with make-believe fantastical features was nothing new. In Britain the shell room had been something of a forerunner of the grotto. At Goodwood, Sussex, Sarah, 2nd Duchess of Richmond, with some help from her daughters, spent seven painstaking years creating a cheerful shell room. Such rooms did not attempt to convey any of the gloom sought by grotto makers. Grottos had, of course, been built in some Renaissance villa gardens in Italy, where they were decorated with fossilised figures, bones and spars to excite sublime, if not horrific, emotion. Alexander Pope can be said to have really started the fashion for building grottos in Britain when in 1720 he constructed the famous grotto in his garden at Twickenham. During that century grottos, follies and hermitages – sometimes with an actual hermit – became must-have features in many aristocratic country house gardens. At Stourhead, a cave created by Henry Hoare included statues of river gods and nymphs.

And yet, outside the sanctuary of country estates belonging to eccentric do-gooders such as Charles Isham and Frank Crisp, gnomes had a tough battle to keep a place. Aesthetically, by the late nineteenth century it was deemed tasteless to have any paint on garden statues (irrespective of the historical fact that the Greeks had painted statues of gods in bright colours). One of the several other reasons why there was resistance towards gnomes was that many hard-working gardeners found the presence of time-wasting gnomes disconcerting and unworthy of approval. Some regarded them as down-right pagan. Indeed, as early as 1712 Alexander Pope, in *The Rape of the Lock*, warned 'The Gnomes, or Dawmons of Earth, delight in mischief'. Moreover, a principal reason for the unacceptability of gnomes was their sedentary proletariat image. Few educated persons wished to be seen to be cluttering their minds by association with the likes of elves, pixies, leprechauns and dwarfs. It was hardly surprising then that the Royal Horticultural Society devised its infamous Article 15, banning from the prestigious Chelsea Flower Show 'highly coloured gnomes, fairies or any similar creatures, actual or mythical for use as garden ornaments'. In 1993 the ban on garden gnomes at Chelsea prompted a demonstration outside the show's main gates. The following year the protestor Michael Ninhall started a rival show in Nottingham – The Ideal Gnome Exhibition.

Ostracised by the horticultural establishment, gnomes lacked respect in the gardening world, and because of pranksters and vandals they could not be conspicuous safely in front gardens. During the 1970s one household in suburban Ealing, which had previously suffered the theft of a prized gnome, was startled to receive through the post an ear of the kidnapped figurine, with a demand for a ransom – 'or else the gnome suffers'!

One response to such victimisation was the creation by Ann Atkin of the Gnome Reserve in North Devon. Recently the group of 2,032 dwarfs on its 4-acre site has been acknowledged by *The Guinness Book of World Records* to be the world's largest collection of gnomes.

Sir Charles Isham, who died in 1903, had by no means been the wastrel his enthusiasm for gnomes implied. He proved to be a

Lamport Hall, Northamptonshire, Isham's stately home. (Charles Isham, *The Wonders of Lamport and the Orphanage Fete*, 1879)

devoted and competent gardener at Lamport Hall: apart from the rockery he successfully created an Italian garden and planted Irish yews to make the Eagle Walk (so called because then it led to a cage of eagles). Also, it was during Isham's time at Lamport that, in 1867, the hall became the scene of what has been described as the most literary find of the nineteenth century: in an attic room was found a trunk that had not been opened for years and that contained a small pile of books of great interest and value. A London bookseller offered Isham a paltry sum for them, but he declined to sell. Some years later, when the library at Lamport was being catalogued, the identification of the books caused a sensation, for among them were first edition folios of Shakespeare, which aroused the interests of experts at the British Museum. Sir Charles eventually made a deal, and today they are prized as part of the collection of the Huntington Library in California.

On the death of his wife, Emily, in 1898, Sir Charles Isham abandoned his beloved garden and retired to Horsham, Sussex. His two surviving daughters disliked the Lamport Hall gnome population, and the elder, Louisa, ordered their removal. Lamport Hall was rented out to a series of hunting tenants until the 1950s when the twelfth baronet, Sir Gyles Isham – a Hollywood actor – set about extensively restoring the hall and its garden. When excavating and recovering the structure of the rockery, one tiny figure found in a crevice appeared to have eluded Louisa's clearance. 'Lampy' the Lamport Gnome, the sole survivor of the 150 eventually imported by Charles Isham, became a highly popular figure and subsequently travelled to Singapore, Australia and New Zealand. The Ishams finally abandoned their ancestral mansion with the death in 1976 of the twelfth baronet, who bequeathed the property to the Lamport Hall Preservation Trust.

Ironically, the Hall's most valued resident now is Lampy, who, as the earliest garden gnome in England, is kept in a glass case in the library, insured for £1 million!

The Gnome Reserve at West Putford, Devon, www.gnomereserve.co.uk; and rockery at Lamport Hall, Northants, www.lamporthall.co.uk.

Christopher Leyland's Monster Tree

Infamous for being the fastest-growing hedge trees, Leyland cypresses can reach heights of 90ft, and are already estimated to number some 55 million in Britain, with many millions more growing in Europe, Australasia and North America. These vigorous conifers threatening to envelop vast areas of suburbia with dense foliage are the subject of passionate disputes and some surprising myths. Dubbed the 'hedge from hell', it is commonly and unjustly assumed to be a virtually Frankenstein-type imported creation. The reality is that, quite by chance, the Leylandii started life in Britain entirely by natural means and in most distinguished circumstances.

Christopher John Leyland was born on 19 September 1849, the first child of John Naylor, who was head of the immensely wealthy Liverpool-based Leyland and Bullin Bank, and whose fortune had originally been made in the slave trade. The Naylor-Leyland family were accustomed to living on an epic scale. Four years before the birth of his son, John Naylor had received as a wedding present Leighton Hall, a 4,000-acre country estate, near

Welshpool in mid-Wales, which he set about extensively transforming into a state-of-the-art mechanised farm. By 1855, on the slopes of the adjoining Long Mountain, he had stocked the park with kangaroos and bison, employed the architect Augustus Pugin to restyle the mansion to house a splendid art collection, built a 100ft observation tower, constructed gigantic farm buildings and equipped the estate with a private funicular railway powered by newfangled mountain stream-fed water-turbines which also drove the estate's sawmills. The estate contained some of the most ingenious feats of engineering of the Victorian age, assembled on a scale unparalleled elsewhere in Britain.

It was here that Christopher Leyland spent his early years. Although much privileged, he and his nine brothers and sisters were unspoilt as children, and were brought up to have a love of nature. Each child, at a young age, was assigned an area of attention on the estate – one sister even developed better strains of hen – and Christopher, being his father's heir apparent, took a good-natured and practical interest in the forestry activities at Leighton Hall. Christopher's mother was President of the Welshpool Horticultural Society and both parents were keen and knowledgeable foresters who since 1855 had been creating one of Britain's earliest redwood pinetums. Soon a variety of specimen trees was growing there, including the Lodgepole pine, giant fir, Wellingtonia and larch. At Leighton Hall, on the edge of the Long Mountain in the Severn valley, conditions were ideal for growing conifers, and the redwood plantation would go on to become one of the most heavily timbered estates of any in Europe. At the neighbouring Herbert family's Powis Castle pinetum eventually would grow Britain's tallest non-native tree – a Douglas fir.

All this while, among the specimen trees in the Leighton Hall pinetum, had been growing a rare Nootka cypress (*Chamaecyparis*

Nookatensis). Only introduced into Britain in 1853 by the Veitchs, it was a robust cedar which was otherwise usually found below the snowlines of the glacial slopes that ranged from Oregon to Alaska. Sometimes also known as the Alaska cedar, it was said to have been named after the Nootka inhabitants of Vancouver Island. Just 50yd to windward in the glade, and also gaining in height, was a Monterey cypress (*Cupressus macrocarpa*) that was otherwise only indigenous to a mile-long stretch of low cliffs near Monterey, California. It was first cultivated in the Royal Horticultural Society's garden at Chiswick in 1838, where it was grown from seed of unknown origin provided by A.B. Lambert. In its natural habitat the Monterey cypress is usually a small, gnarled, twisted tree.

Christopher Leyland, who appeared to be a villain because of his Leylandii tree, was a maritime hero who funded the creation of the revolutionary steam-turbine engine. (*North News & Pictures*)

These two types of tree would normally never meet in their wild habitat, which was thousands of miles apart. Natural crossbreeding was a rare occurrence in plants, particularly in conifers. Furthermore, these parent species belonged to quite different sections of the genus. Nevertheless, a cross occurred in the Leighton pinetum when the female flowers of the Nootka cypress were fertilised by pollen from the Monterey cypress. Quite unaware of this, in 1888 Christopher Leyland gathered and sowed seeds which he had found on a cone from the Nootka. Later he glanced at the fledgling seedlings and noticed that six of them differed slightly from the rest. Had he destroyed them the history of trees would have been none the wiser, but, such was nature's fortune (or misfortune, some neighbours might now think), he had a tolerant heart and chose to spare them.

Christopher's life was nearing a transformation stage. Although he inherited Leighton Hall from his father in 1889, the following year his wife of 15 years also died. Then, in 1891, so too did a great-uncle, who bequeathed him another huge estate, the 23,000-acre Haggerston Castle, near Berwick-upon-Tweed, in Northumberland. Resolved to make a fresh start Christopher left Leighton Hall in favour of his next brother and moved to Northumberland, where he made Haggerston his personal residence and spent the next few years extensively rebuilding it. To the house he attached a huge glass conservatory to accommodate his personal collection of unusual plant life. The six Leylandii seedlings he brought with him from Leighton Hall, were planted in 1892 in the garden at Haggerston. Continuing his parents' arboricultural experiments, during the rest of his life he is said to have planted millions of trees (only a few of which were Leylandii) in the Kyloe Woods section of the huge estate.

In 1862 Christopher Leyland entered the Royal Navy, where he served for ten years before retiring as a sub-lieutenant. He then held an investment position in the family bank, and – perhaps because he possessed some unusual knowledge of turbines gained from those functioning on the Leighton Hall estate – he began giving financial advice to the steam-turbine innovator Charles Parsons. From his father, who had been a keen yachtsman and a member of the Royal Yacht Squadron, Christopher also acquired a deep love of the sea. And, from another relative, ship owner Frederick Richard Leyland (the head of the Leyland Line) Christopher appreciated the commercial opportunities for developing nautical technology. By 1894 he was the main financial investor in, and a director of, the Parsons Marine Steam Turbine Co. Around the lake at Haggerston were towed, by fishing line, hull models of the test vessel, which was due to be powered by the revolutionary engines. *Turbinia*, the sea-going prototype version, of which Leyland became captain, became the fastest vessel afloat, and Christopher made maritime history by audaciously demonstrating its phenomenal 36-knot speed at the 1897 Spithead Naval Review.

Meanwhile, as the six seedlings brought from Welshpool grew, it became evident to Christopher that they were the result of a natural cross. Quietly delighted by the discovery, and without telling anyone beyond the confines of his family, he named the creation Leyland cypress (*Cupressocyparis leylandii*). He allowed cuttings to be taken of the trees and distributed to various woods on the estate. Yet in 1911 there was another extraordinary occurrence at Leighton Hall. Leyland's nephew, Captain J.M. Naylor, found a cone, this time from a Monterey cypress growing 50yd from a Nootka. Two seedlings of this batch appeared different from the rest, and mindful of Uncle Christopher's 1888 discovery, Naylor had them planted out. Fourteen years later he noted they had grown to 28ft high, whereas a Monterey cypress from the same seedbed had reached just 21ft. Evidently the Leyland cypress not only grew faster than either of its parents, it was promising to grow far higher.

The outside world only got to hear of the existence of the burgeoning monster trees at Leighton Hall and Haggerston because in July 1925 a tree specialist – who had perchance visited Leighton Hall – sent a sample of the hitherto unseen foliage to the Botanical Gardens at Kew. News of the discovery, which was hailed as 'One of the most important tree introductions of recent times', was broken to the public in the *Kew Bulletin* in autumn 1926. Then, in 1940, Leylandii seedlings appeared in a garden at Ferndown, Dorset, and were then sown in the nurseries of M. Barthelemy, at Stapehill. Significantly that made it apparent that where the right parent trees were in the same place natural hybridisation could occur. From the various Leylandii seeds and cuttings taken by Kew Gardens to produce stock-plants were eventually derived eight varieties of Leyland cypress, with names such as Naylor's Blue, Haggerston Grey and Leighton Green. From these in turn were grown clones that were distributed worldwide.

Largest International Arboretums

Name	Where	Acres
Holden Arboretum	Cleveland, USA	3,400
Mount Auburn Cemetery	Boston, USA	2,500
Morton Arboretum	Illinois, USA	1,700
Westonbirt Arboretum	Tetbury, UK	600
US National Arboretum	Washington DC, USA	446

A beauty of the Leyland cypress was that it seemed to possess all the virtues for which the Monterey cypress had been so widely planted – and none of its vices. Like the Monterey it was resistant to sea winds. Whereas the Monterey was restricted to milder climates, the Leyland cypress inherited from its other parent the ability to resist the worst of most winters without damage. It was capable of being a fine specimen tree and also a reliable and fast-growing shelterbelt tree. Moreover, surely it would make an excellent hedge plant? Its ability to withstand such restriction was shown by the flourishing dwarf hedges in the arboretum nursery at Kew. Planted in 1947, the hedges were kept down by drastic mechanical trimming to a height of 4ft, and reportedly showed no resentment of such drastic treatment.

For many gardeners the practicalities of trimming the Leyland cypress were less of a priority than its attraction as a fast-growing hedge that could take to almost any soil. Nurserymen pushed it as a sales item because they could grow it easily and therefore sell it cheaply, and in enormous numbers. Then along came the supermarkets, and other large retail outlets, who also realised how much profit could be made out of the Leyland cypress. In fact it was singularly unsuited for the purpose of hedging in all but the largest of sites. Though chosen for hedge planting because it could produce an effective hedge in three to five years, few people who bought the Leyland understood that it could grow into an uncontrollable 'beanstalk'. Indeed, the Leyland cypress could well reach heights of 138ft!

Houseowners soon found controlling the tree an onerous annual chore. If the trimming of the sides was neglected for a short while, the rapid growth meant it would be necessary to cut back into the old wood. That would leave ugly dead sticks that would never produce leaves again. The dry heart of the tree was

The first Leyland cyprus was discovered in 1888 in the grounds of Leighton Hall, Christopher Leyland's birthplace near Welshpool. Widely sold and praised for decades as a fast-growing hedge tree that became densely foliated and capable of reaching heights of 138ft, the Leyland cyprus grew to become Britain's most infamous nuisance tree. (Forestry Commission)

extremely flammable and if planted close to a house these hedges constituted a fire hazard. If allowed to grow naturally, the tree was apt to lose the lower branches in heavy snow, and this could result in tall but very scruffy-looking hedges. It was even inhospitable to wildlife, since it offered virtually nothing in terms of food. The Leyland cypress's reputation as a nuisance 'hedge from hell' became apparent in the 1990s because of various celebrated legal wrangles between petty-minded neighbours squabbling over root-caused damage and natural light blocked by untrimmed growth.

Belgium, France, Germany, Holland and Switzerland have all found it necessary to introduce hedge-nuisance legislation. Ironically, because it is not a naturally occurring plant, the Leyland cypress has been grown far and wide, and in New Zealand and Australia it is used for wood products. Rooting cuttings arrived in the United States, through California, for the first time in 1941. Then in 1965 they found their way to South Carolina where their potential for use as Christmas trees became apparent to the State Forestry Commission and private growers. For that purpose, and as a valued landscape plant, it has been successfully grown in California, Louisiana, Mississippi, Alabama, Georgia, Florida and the Carolinas.

Oblivious to the mayhem he was storing up for future generations, Christopher Leyland lived out his final years as a keen member of the Royal Yacht Squadron. At Parsons he became a national hero as the captain of the world's first steam-turbine ship, the *Turbinia*. Parsons's revolutionary steam turbines went on to power transatlantic liners such as the *Titanic*. Ashore, Christopher Leyland cared greatly for the welfare of his numerous tenants and had the reputation of being one of the fairest landlords. In October 1926, within weeks of the *Kew Bulletin*'s revelation, he died at Haggerston Castle. He took with him the still unresolved mystery of how before 1888 the parent trees of the Leyland cypress got to the Leighton Hall pinetum from North America.

See the National Pinetum at Bedgebury, Kent. Christopher Leyland's world-famous demonstration steam-turbine ship *Turbinia* is on display at the Discovery Museum, Blandford Square, Newcastle-upon-Tyne.

John Manning's Prefab Shed

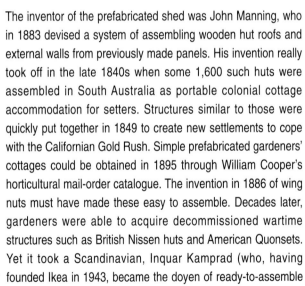

The inventor of the prefabricated shed was John Manning, who in 1883 devised a system of assembling wooden hut roofs and external walls from previously made panels. His invention really took off in the late 1840s when some 1,600 such huts were assembled in South Australia as portable colonial cottage accommodation for setters. Structures similar to those were quickly put together in 1849 to create new settlements to cope with the Californian Gold Rush. Simple prefabricated gardeners' cottages could be obtained in 1895 through William Cooper's horticultural mail-order catalogue. The invention in 1886 of wing nuts must have made these easy to assemble. Decades later, gardeners were able to acquire decommissioned wartime structures such as British Nissen huts and American Quonsets. Yet it took a Scandinavian, Inquar Kamprad (who, having founded Ikea in 1943, became the doyen of ready-to-assemble furniture), to make gardeners confident enough to enable flat-pack garden sheds to become commonplace.

William Harcourt's Country House Demolitions

The restoration of the lost gardens, including the famous 'lost' garden at Heligan in recent years, has brought to public attention the consequences of the so-called country house crisis of decades ago with the extinction of many horticultural gems. During the twentieth century hundreds of country house gardens were lost forever as a consequence of death duties, regardless of the heroically innovative financial and practical measures later devised to save them.

Death duties, the punitive wealth tax that came to have such a devastating impact on Britain's immense stock of country houses and gardens, was established in 1894 by the Liberal Chancellor of the Exchequer, Sir William Harcourt. Tall and jovial, Sir William was a somewhat raffish character, who had an unfortunate trait of enjoying personal vendettas more than battles of principle. The landed Harcourt dynasty from which he descended had arrived in Britain with the Normans and established a track record of callous property dealings. From 1755 their most spectacular residence was Nuneham Courtenay, a fine Palladian mansion on a hill by the Thames. To provide stone foundations for this building the 1st Viscount Harcourt, who at the time was Lord Chancellor to Queen Anne, in 1755 pulled down much of Stanton Harcourt, his ancestral fourteenth-century home near Oxford, irrespective of its being one of the earliest unfortified manor houses in England. Four years later, to improve the view at Nuneham Courtenay the 1st Viscount moved the entire village of Cokethorpe to a new site outside the park. The effect was such that the grounds were later described by Horace Walpole – perhaps with some exaggeration – as 'one of the most beautiful landscapes in the world'. But the scandalous removal of the village and the transformation of its medieval church into a Greek temple were made infamous by Oliver Goldsmith's immortal poem 'The Deserted Village' (1770), a polemic against the social damage wrought by such landscaping.

Born into the heart of the English establishment in 1827, William Harcourt both exemplified and challenged this world. From his earliest years he feuded with his elder brother, Edward, whose future inheritance of Nuneham Courtenay he resented. When first standing for Parliament in 1859 as an independent Liberal against a local Liberal grandee, Harcourt argued the seat needed to be wrenched from local 'hereditary rights'. By 1893 William was Chancellor of the Exchequer and raised income tax from 6*d* to 7*d*. That year a Home Rule Bill was passed in the House of Commons but was crushingly defeated by the Lords. Harcourt, joining the general Liberal condemnation of the Lords for failing to pass the bill (and causing Gladstone's resignation) reckoned he was next in line to be prime minister; but the job went to his rival, Lord Rosebery. Harcourt then plotted his revenge on the privileged landed class. On overcoming fierce parliamentary opposition to his so-called death duties budget, William secured approval for the 1894 Finance Act which brought into being a tax known as estate duty. Replacing the traditionally mild probate duty, Harcourt's new scheme imposed an incremental scale of charges which rose to death duties at 8 per cent on estates of £2 million or more. In the preparation of the duties Rosebery had cautioned Harcourt to make allowances for deaths comparatively close to one another; but Harcourt, in a move which would later haunt his relatives, declined.

Already the economic reality was that many country estates were struggling. Despite the end of the 1873–92 Great Depression in agriculture, farming was at a low ebb and thus upper-class families who were entirely dependent on an income from farming found themselves in financial difficulties, which meant that the money spent on necessary maintenance of country houses and gardens was reduced. The condition of such gardens worsened during, and as a consequence of, the First World War, when many gardeners – such as those from Heligan – perished in battle or returned, when the conflict ceased, unwilling to re-enter domestic service. Another significant factor that led to the decline of the country house and garden was the disproportionately high losses of officers during the First World War. Heirs had become subalterns, and the average life span for a subaltern in Flanders was a few months. Of the titled families almost one in ten lost the direct heir to their estates during this war, and the demise of a direct heir often meant doom for a country house. Death duty impositions were further increased in Lloyd George's 1909 People's Budget and also in the 1919 budget, which made estates of £2 million and over liable to death duties of 40 per cent. That year, when the promise went out for 'homes for heroes', few were

Sir William Harcourt. (Mary Evans Picture Library)

in the mood to be concerned about what happened to country houses and their fine gardens.

With estates overburdened by death duties country houses had to be sold and subsequently demolished. In *The Destruction of the Country House* John Harris claims that 'the holocaust of 1914–18 was to herald the death of over four hundred houses. Month after month occurred that dreadful series of demolitions. It was comparable to the Reformation, and the sadness is that it was not necessary.' The search for a means of preventing such demolition had begun as early as 1877 with the founding by William Morris of the Society for the Protection of Ancient Buildings. Though well meaning, the SPAB could do little but protest, as it did famously in 1929 with a poster campaign against Randolph Hurst's secret dismantling in Wiltshire of the medieval Bradenstoke Priory.

An organisation that had better prospects of saving the country houses thrown into peril by Sir William Harcourt's death duty scheme was the National Trust, which – also in 1894 – had been founded by the philanthropic social reformer Octavia Hill (1838–1912), Sir Robert Hunter and Canon Rawnsley. In 1907 an Act of Parliament was passed enabling the Trust to hold properties permanently and 'for the benefit of the nation'. However, by the early 1930s it had succeeded only in acquiring a few properties, most notably Montacute and Barrington Castle. With only 1,000 subscribers the Trust simply could not afford to take on the great houses whose futures hung in the balance. In 1934, Lord Lothian, the British Ambassador to the United States, ominously forewarned the Trust: 'Most of these country houses are now under sentence of death, and the axe which is destroying them is taxation, and especially that form of taxation known as death duties. I do not think it an exaggeration that within a generation, hardly one of these historic houses will be lived in by the families who created them.'

By 1945 the prospects for the nation's private country houses had worsened still further. During the Second World War some had suffered bomb damage and many had been requisitioned, either as refuges for civilian evacuees, or used as barracks and thus their grounds detailed for military training purposes. Even the Harcourt family could not escape these disruptions – their riverside Nuneham Park was requisitioned and then misused by the RAF. Nor did there seem to be any significant compensation to other country house owners for the damage carelessly inflicted by such wartime occupants. Furthermore, the Attlee government saw to it that on some country estates the death duties could be as high as 80 per cent.

In 1937 new legislation came into being enabling certain properties that were handed over to the National Trust to be exempt from estate duty. The Trust charged the historian James Lees-Milne (the Secretary of their Country House Committee) to negotiate with struggling owners: the trust was by now inundated with pleas for financial salvation. Lees-Milne toured far and wide, and his opinion could literally mean life or death to an estate. All too often the scene that greeted him on those peregrinations was grimly familiar: a mansion so dilapidated it was only partially habitable, yet was home to threadbare gentry with virtually no prospect of sufficient income. Sometimes the houses and grounds were failed showpieces that had only been in existence since the nineteenth-century country house boom, with no architectural merit and already falling apart. Especially unfortunate for such cases were Lees-Milne's priorities, which were never directed to the well-being of the occupants, only to the worthiness of the building. In the absence of his endorsement country houses, and with them their gardens, were being bulldozed, almost at the rate of one a week.

The remedy appeared in the pages of *Country Life* in November 1945 when the Marchioness of Exeter wrote the first in a series of articles on 'The Future of Great Country Houses'. She called for tax remission in respect of maintenance and repairs, and the cost of staff to look after the contents: 'it is the houses and their irreplaceable contents that require staff, not the personal needs of their owner-residents'. In his concluding article Christopher Hussey called for a system like that used by the French government, who provided 50 per cent grants towards the upkeep of the great châteaux. According to Roy Strong's book *The English Arcadia*, the Attlee administration was to prove far less philistine to the cause of the great house than the Conservatives had been. In 1937 the Labour Chancellor, Stafford Cripps, pragmatically made it possible for estates to be exempted from death duties if they were handed over to the National Trust.

These new rules revitalised the National Trust and enabled it to take on many more properties, which eventually included historic gardens such as Hidcote, Nymans and the derelict Westbury Court. However, a difficulty facing Ellen Field, who in the immediate years after the Second World War became the Trust's first Gardens Adviser, was the scarcity of know-how of restoration techniques. The first restoration of a garden in Britain had, in fact, been effected in 1810–13 by Alexander Forbes, who repaired Guillaume Beaumont's famous seventeenth-century formal garden at Levens Hall. Although in 1935 George Chettle had innovatively applied archaeological methods to excavating the shaped beds outside Kirby Hall, Northamptonshire, such deliberate reconstructions were still far from commonplace.

Heroic though the National Trust was in saving such horticultural treasures from the clutches of the Inland Revenue, it has been criticised for its sometimes clumsy conservation of historic gardens. Particularly at fault was Graham Stuart Thomas, who, following Ellen Field's early death in 1955, served as its Gardens Adviser until 1974 when he became a consultant. Stuart Thomas was of the Arts and Crafts planting design tradition, and controversially – albeit restrained by limited funding – instead of properly restoring gardens, tended to smother them with mulch. However, Stuart Thomas was the instigator by trial and error of large-scale garden conservation in Britain, and when he retired in 1974 his successor, John Sales, could go on to restore some 170 gardens for the National Trust. By acquiring many more stately homes and gardens on large landed estates the Trust eventually possessed, according to Stuart Thomas's estimate, the 'biggest horticultural collection' in one ownership in Britain, and possibly anywhere in the world. Indeed, the National Trust's good example spread overseas: in the United States, where more than two-thirds of great American gardens had already been lost, the Garden Conservancy was founded as an organisation devoted to garden preservation.

In 1948 Stafford Cripps appointed a committee under Sir Ernest Gowers to consider the situation regarding privately owned country houses and gardens that were unlikely to be accepted by the National Trust. Crucially the 1950 Gowers Report, 'The Country House Charter', recommended the government intervene to give incentives and relief to those fortunate, and unfortunate, enough to be owners of historic houses. In fact, tax remission to country house owners never did materialise. What, perhaps unintentionally, did save country houses were generous farm subsidy incomes, which, if invested wisely, supplied the owners with just enough means to survive the death duty storms.

A consequence of the Gowers Report was the creation in 1953 of the Historic Buildings Council, which listed houses and made grants towards restoration. Gardens too – most notably those which were classed as Grade 1 – became listed; and, in the 1980s Whitehall rather belatedly endorsed a *Register of Parks and Gardens of Special Historic Interest*. Concern for the well-being of such treasures caused the conservation group SAVE Britain's Heritage to publish *Elysian Gardens* (1978); and, even earlier, in 1965 the founding of the scholarly Garden History Society.

Sir William Harcourt could never have envisaged that one consequence of his 1894 death duties would be, a hundred years later, the growth of a National Trust whose 3 million members (the largest civilian membership organisation in Western Europe) wished to see a continuance of the houses and gardens, the ownership of which he had seemed so keen to weaken. Had he ever intended that his own family should suffer from his punitive inheritance tax? His elder brother, Edward, died in 1891, to be followed by his only son in March 1904, who had no heir: Sir William then inherited the family's Stanton Harcourt and Nuneham Park in an impoverished estate. Perhaps the financial shock was too much, because that October William also died. Burdened by the death duties Sir William had established, and with no compensation to repair the damage incurred during the Second World War, in 1948 the remaining Harcourts moved to Stanton Harcourt and were forced to sell Nuneham Park. The family had lost their fateful mansion on the hill forever.

Nuneham Park is now the Global Retreat Centre, www.bksu.org.uk; its woodlands are run separately as the Harcourt Aboretum, www.oxtrust.org.uk.

Guillaume Beaumont's Ha-ha

The ha-ha enabled persons within eighteenth-century country gardens to have an uninterrupted view of the surrounding parklands, while cattle, sheep and other livestock were kept out. This ingeniously simple revolutionary device consisted of a dry ditch with a steep slope and vertical wall built to ground level. It proved ideal for giving clear views along *allées* and across *parterres*, and even meant gaps in walls could be livestock-proof. Reputedly it derived from the deep military style trenches André Le Notre had ordered to be dug for landscape purposes at Versailles. An evolution of the ha-ha was the *saut de loup* ('jump of the wolf'), a sunken fence first constructed in England in 1694–5 at Levens Hall, Cumbria, by Guillaume Beaumont, the French head gardener there. Printed descriptions of the ha-ha initially appeared in English in 1712 when John James translated a 1709 work of Dezallier d'Argenville's as *The Theory and Practice of Gardening*. The earliest British landscape architect to make extensive use of the device was Charles Bridgeman, who in 1724 at Blenheim built one of Cotswold stone a mile long. Being practically invisible until up close, the contrivance could be perilous for horseriders – and also the socially unwary. According to Horace Walpole, son of the first prime minister, 'common people' exclaimed 'Aha' to express surprise at suddenly finding an unperceived check to their walk, whereas knowing gentry would laugh 'Haha' when others unwittingly fell into it!

The ha-ha. (J.C. Loudon (ed.), *The Landscape Gardening and Landscape Architecture of the late Humphrey Repton*, Longman, 1840)

Most Common Garden Birds in the UK

Bird	Average Per Garden
Common sparrow	4.56
Starling	3.63
Blue tit	2.9
Blackbird	2.42
Greenfinch	1.83
Chaffinch	1.83
Collared dove	1.51
Wood pigeon	1.51
Great tit	1.39
Robin	1.28

(Birdwatch 2005, *The Guardian*, 21 March 2005)

Paul Muller's DDT Insecticide

A seemingly wondrous insecticide devised in 1939 by the Swiss chemist Paul Hermann Muller unforeseeably became an environmental *bête noire* and thence had a revolutionary effect on attitudes towards the use of chemicals in gardens.

Hitherto, many gardens sported potting shed shelves like a hypochondriac's medicine cupboard. Fearsome garden pesticides had increasingly been used over the course of several centuries. In 1594 the aristocratic Bethnal Green inventor Sir Hugh Platt (1552–1608) produced *The Jewel House of Art and Nature*, listing various horticultural improvements he had devised, including salt and marl fertilisers, and a lead-based insecticide for disposing of wasps. In the nineteenth century lime sulphur and, later,

Bordeaux mixture were the main fungicides. In 1866 the RHS lobbied the government to rescind the duty on tobacco if imported for horticultural fumigation purposes (a matter 'of the greatest importance'). Another popular means of killing insects in greenhouses, or tents specially placed over fruit trees, was to use cyanide gas, which was activated by dropping cyanide salt into a shallow bath. Spraying usually consisted of applying a mist of tar distillates by means of ingenious devices, ranging from syringes to pneumatic spraying machines. To dispense sulphur powder insecticides, such as Green Paris, bellows would be used. The health hazards to gardeners of thus treating edible garden produce – usually without any form of personal protection – were never seriously contemplated. In the 1930s the main concern with pesticides was not their composition, but their availability. Thus, when in 1931 the Pharmaceutical Society lobbied for an amendment to the Pharmacy and Poisons Bill, making chemists responsible for the sale of pesticides, the RHS only campaigned against it to protect the livelihoods of nursery businesses.

Brilliant though Paul Muller's discovery was, the substance which came to have the astonishing name of dichlorodiphenyl-trichloethane (DDT) had originally been made as a compound many years earlier. In 1874 a German chemistry student called Othmar Zeidler, working at the laboratory of Adolph von Bayer at the University of Strasbourg, first synthesised the compound. He made hundreds of other compounds, but, unconcerned to suggest any uses for them, failed to realise DDT's value as an insecticide; nor did he receive any particular attention for the work he had done. In 1925 Paul Muller (1899–1965), who was born in Olten, Switzerland, received his doctorate and began working as an industrial research chemist at the J.R. Geigy Company, Basel. There he developed vegetable dyes and natural tanning agents,

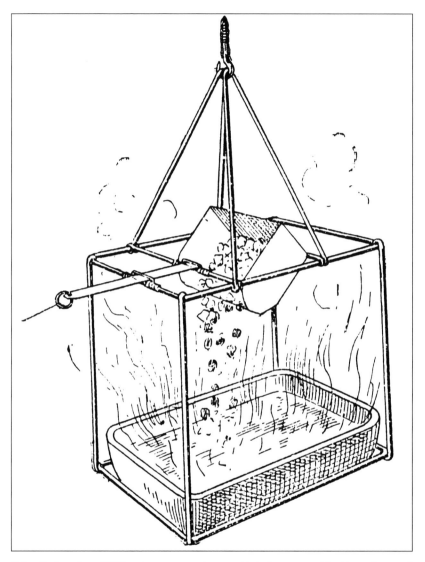

Before the invention of DDT, various means, such as cyanide baths, were used to rid greenhouses of insects. (Hooper Pearson, *The Book of Garden Pests*, John Lane, 1908)

mothproofing agents for textiles, a mercury-free seed disinfectant, before, in 1935 he began to search for an ideal synthetic insecticide. He wanted one that would show rapid, potent toxicity for the greatest number of insect species but would cause little or no damage to plants and warm-blooded animals. He also required the product to have a high degree of chemical stability, so that its effect would persist for long periods of time and manufacture would be economical. After four years of experiments Muller rediscovered and tested the DDT that Othmar Zeidler had abandoned in 1874, and found it met the necessary requirements.

In 1939 DDT was tested successfully against the Colorado potato beetle by the Swiss government. Further field trials showed it also to be effective against a wide variety of pests, including the common housefly, louse and mosquito. Two products based on DDT, Gesarol and Neocide, were marketed in 1942, and small quantities were covertly shipped to the United States, where in 1943 they were tested by the US Department of Agriculture. At the time Allied supplies of the best available alternative, pyrethrum (which had been in use since ancient times), were running dangerously low, so in New Jersey an initial batch of 500lb was hastily made by Merck & Company by duplicating Zeidler's 1874 procedure! In January 1944 it was rushed by truck to an airport, then flown to Italy where it was used to quash an outbreak of typhus body lice in Naples. Allied troops were dusted with DDT powder and an estimated 5,000 lives were saved. It was the first time a winter typhus epidemic had been stopped. Further batches were made then dispatched to Guadalcanal in the South Pacific, where US troops were suffering badly from malaria. The effect there of Muller's DDT, which virtually eliminated malaria immediately, won the praise of Winston Churchill, who described it as 'excellent DDT powder'. Later in 1943 the US Army issued small tin boxes of DDT dust to all its troops. DDT contributed to the belief that the Second World War was the first major conflict in which more combatants died from action than from disease. Perhaps if Othmar Zeidler had made an insecticide out of his 1874 findings German losses in the trenches – soldiers were ravaged by insect-borne disease in the First World War – might have been fewer and the course of history might thus have been altered.

Cleared for civilian application in 1945, DDT was adopted by national health programmes and also the World Health Organisation. In Greece it showed spectacular results in the fight against malaria, the number of victims falling from some 2 million each year to a mere 5,000 by 1951. DDT was especially successful in enabling malaria to be virtually eradicated from

Paul Muller, winner of a Nobel Prize for discovering DDT. (Mary Evans Picture Library)

101

many island areas. Ceylon (later Sri Lanka) was a famous success: in the 1950s there were more that 12,000 deaths there annually; by 1963, none at all. Estimates for the number of lives DDT saved from malaria between 1945 and 1971 vary between 60 million and 500 million – throughout 27 countries. Additionally, entire nations were rid of deadly pests that spread fatal diseases such as plague, yellow fever and typhus.

What made DDT seem so wonderful a pesticide was its apparent ability to do everything. It lacked water solubility, unlike other pesticides of its time, it did not wash away in the rain and was resistant to sunlight decomposition. It killed a large variety of insects without, it was believed, harming mammals or birds. And it was inexpensive to produce. At the time the RHS pathologist at Wisley, George Fox-Wilson, was slightly more sceptical about its merits and cautiously reported: 'The fact that these preparations [specifically DDT] are toxic to beneficial insects renders it necessary to time their application with care.' Undeterred, British gardeners became keen purchasers of insecticides containing DDT, especially for greenhouse use. When used on allotments, yields improved markedly. In arboriculture it was found that DDT could be sprayed on to healthy elms in order to kill Dutch elm disease beetles before they could introduce the disease into the trees. With DDT seemingly having no harmful side effects, Paul Muller became a scientific hero. In 1948, to honour his achievement in discovering the potent toxic effects of DDT on insects, he was awarded the Nobel Prize for Medicine.

However, the credibility of DDT was dealt a shattering blow in June 1962 when the *New Yorker* magazine commenced a series of articles by the ecologist Rachel Carson. Hitherto no one had thought there might be a pattern to the occasional appearance of obscure scientific reports indicating that all might not be well with

DDT. As early as 1946 the *Journal of Economic Entomology* had speculated about the possible threat of DDT to mammals, birds and fish. From Illinois had come in 1958 a description of robins poisoned by eating earthworms that had ingested DDT in leaves under elms sprayed to control Dutch elm disease.

Carson was in a unique position to pull together various pieces of hitherto uncoordinated evidence. A renowned nature author, she had been an eminent marine biologist with the US Fish and Wildlife Service. In her brilliant and controversial 1962 book *Silent Spring*, Carson brought her training as a biologist and her skill as a writer to bear with great force on a significant, and

In the 1950s many garden chemicals contained DDT. (*Gardeners' Chronicle*, 6 June 1953)

103

DDT could be applied in greenhouses by smoke devices. (*Gardeners' Chronicle*, 11 April 1959)

seemingly sinister, aspect of technological progress. *Silent Spring* was a story of the use of toxic chemicals in the country-side and of the widespread des-truction of wildlife in America. Claiming humans were also at risk because DDT was stored in fat deposits that entered the body, Carson cited a claim made by a scientific team from the US Public Health Service who sampled restaurant and institu-tional meals and found that each one contained DDT. She accused the food industry of playing down the existence of chemical residues in the food Americans ate.

'Gardening', Carson insisted, 'is now firmly linked with the super-poisons' such as DDT. 'Little is done to warn the gar-dener or home owner that he is handling extremely dangerous materials.' On the contrary, almost every newspaper's gar-dening page and the majority of gardening magazines took their use for granted, and 'Those who fail to make use of this array of lethal sprays and dust are by implication remiss.' Yet warnings on labels were printed so inconspicuously that few took the trouble to read or follow them. She cited the case of an American physician – an enthusiastic spare-time gardener – who had begun to spray DDT regularly every week on his shrubs and lawn. In doing so his skin often became soaked with spray. After a year of such activity he suddenly collapsed and was hospitalised. Tests done on fat specimens revealed heavy accumulations of DDT. There had been extensive nerve damage.

Carson's campaign succeeded in making a villain of DDT – and by association the well-meaning Paul Muller who had devised it – and by the late 1960s the United Nations had effectively banned its use. In gardens this meant that birds and insects were now spared from being harmed by ingesting foliage treated with DDT. However, several years later the banning of DDT was seen as a cause of the dramatic rise of outbreaks of malaria and millions of deaths in countries where hitherto it had been so effective. Many scientists accused Carson – who by then had died of cancer – of having been a scaremonger. In sparing the well-being of wildlife and gardeners she had contributed to the deaths of millions of persons who were less well off.

The Rachel Carson Homestead, an environmental centre in Springdale, Pennsylvania, www.rachelcarson.org.

John Innes's Peat Compost

For decades gardeners have continued to use John Innes's and others' peat composts to enhance their gardens' productivity, seemingly oblivious to the passionate controversy in recent years about how the extraction of peat compost has been damaging the British Isles' peatlands. In fact, the renown and popularity of John Innes composts has meant the character whose name appears on those bags was unwittingly partly responsible for the destructive peat extraction bonanza. Before the 1930s composts had traditionally been mixed by gardeners using their own recipes.

John Innes (1829–1904) amassed a fortune as a property developer. From his earliest years he was brought up in London with a sense of business and public duty: his father was the author of reports to the government on the West Indies and the abolition of slavery, and his mother was the daughter of a Member of Parliament. Initially, John was a wine importer, with premises in the City of London. Then, in 1864, he co-founded (with his brother James) the City of London Real Property Company. From the mid-1860s the brothers acquired land, including several farms, in Merton and Morden, Surrey, some 8 miles south of Westminster. John Innes reconstructed as a working farm the farmhouse of Manor Farm, Merton, and turned it into the Manor House, which in 1867 became his home. He became more concerned with developing what was to be Merton Park, an early garden estate centred on the old village, around the church of St Mary the Virgin, building houses there between the early 1870s and 1904. Merton Park Estate, perhaps the first example of the 'garden suburb', was begun in 1871. Modest houses with their own grounds were intended to reflect the spirit of the English country estate, to be bought by City workers who wanted good rail links to the metropolis and some semblance of rural life. The estate did not develop as far as planned during Innes's lifetime, although he achieved an idyllic effect with wide avenues and holly hedges. Lower Merton railway station was renamed Merton Park.

In 1872 Innes became lord of the manor of Merton. By then, according to a later obituary in the *Wimbledon News*, he was 'somewhat stern in his demeanour, but generous'. A considerable local philanthropist, he supported the charities and churches of Merton and Morden. Enlightened though Innes was towards providing good quality commuter housing, he was also concerned by the changes industrialisation was having on the living environment. In fact he was so discriminatory in his support for new technology that he campaigned against bicycles, and later the motor car! When he died in 1904 he bequeathed an estate of £325,000, and for the purposes of establishing an experimental 'school of horticulture' he donated his Manor House at Merton and 5 acres of adjacent farmland, together with workshops, scientific apparatus, libraries, and lecture halls. In 1910, six years after his death, the John Innes Horticultural Institution was established, employing several of Innes's former labourers. Also, the John Innes Park, a public park, was opened in the grounds of the Manor House.

The Charity Commissioners described the aims of the institute as 'to carry out investigations, whether of a scientific or practical nature'. Accordingly, in the years subsequent to its foundation, the John Innes Horticultural Institution strove to advance the science of horticulture. It became Britain's earliest research institute for plant breeding and genetics. In the 1930s two of the institution's scientists, William Lawrence and John Newell, set out to formulate a range of composts that would provide consistently good and reliable results. The main elements for virtually all composts, they calculated, were loam, peat and sand (together with some fertiliser mixture). Having undertaken many careful plant pot experiments they found that by altering the proportions of the elements they could recommend just six basic recipes of compost to cover virtually the entire range of British horticultural composting requirements. The John Innes Horticultural Institution did not commercially produce the composts itself in its own factories. What it did do was allow its recipes and reputable name to be used by manufacturers. The result, for ordinary gardeners in the 1930s, was that for the first time standardised seed and potting composts became commercially available. Many professional and amateur gardeners reported better and more reliable yields from the John Innes composts. Unfortunately, the success of these

John Innes's revolutionary preformed composts created a demand for peat. (John Innes Foundation, courtesy of the John Innes Trustees)

products enabled a belief to develop that just one of its least expensive elements – peat – was by itself a reliable means of making plants grow better.

Peat consists of partly decomposed plant remains, and can include sphagnum moss, trees, shrubs, herbs, grasses, reeds and sedges. It forms where plant debris is added faster than it is broken down. Thus it forms best when the natural processes of decay are arrested by natural acid – such as by waterlogging and the exclusion of oxygen, whereby the remains of succeeding wetland plants become compacted to form peat. Peat itself is not especially nutritious, however. William Lawrence's book *The Fruit, the Seed and the Soil*, published in 1954, reported, 'The value of peat in a compost is as a soil "conditioner". Its spongy nature makes it unique: it can aerate compost and regulate its moisture-holding qualities at one and the same time.' Nevertheless he went on to report that peat was also 'naturally highly sterile'. Lawrence's cautious comments were subsequently ignored amid increasing demands by consumers to have inexpensive supplies of peat.

Attempts to use peat for horticultural purposes were not entirely new. Near Stranraer, in 1939, many blocks of it were assembled to form a showpiece peat garden at the Royal Botanic Gardens, Logan. What really made gardeners develop a habit for using composting peat was the selling at British nurseries in the 1960s of huge and inexpensive green polythene-wrapped bales labelled 'shamrock peat'. Costing some 10 shillings, these enormous 80-litre bales seemed a low-cost means of instantly adding improvement to a garden. Unfortunately, the peat was fairly dry, because it was often used for scattering on ornamental beds, and much of it was blown away by the wind. Grow-bags, which first became available to amateur gardeners in 1973, were revolutionary. They could provide the basis of a simple balcony garden,

Lawrence Hills' Organic Movement

The most influential pioneer of the modern organic gardening movement was a freelance journalist called Lawrence Hills. In the early 1950s, while researching the value of comfrey as a crop, Hills learnt of Henry Doubleday (1813–1902), a Quaker entrepreneur who had owned a glue factory and introduced Russian comfrey into Britain in the hope it would provide glue for the new penny black stamp. Despite the glue's failure – and the consequent sale of the factory – Doubleday had recognised comfrey's potential to be an exceptionally prolific source of protein and devoted the rest of his life to studying and popularising this wonder plant. By 1958 Hills decided to establish a charitable organisation, the Henry Doubleday Research Association (HDRA), to study the uses of comfrey and, more significantly, to develop methods for growing plants organically. In those early years he rented an acre of land at Bocking, near Braintree in Essex, funding it by writing articles for the *Observer*. HDRA was conceived as a club for experimenting gardeners, and by 1974 the growth of enthusiasm for organic gardening required Hills to employ as helpers Alan and Jackie Gear, who moved HDRA to a new site at Ryton-on-Dunsmore. Jackie Gear was particularly determined to shed the organic movement's cranky luddite image, and by 2002 had succeeded in bringing it into the horticultural mainstream when HDRA was renamed Garden Organic.

and allowed suburban gardeners to grow tomatoes easily. Not only did they become increasingly commonplace in garden centres, supermarkets and even petrol stations, they made gardeners more familiar with the fairly new concept of multipurpose peat-based compost, which further increased the need to extract yet more peat. An even greater boost to demand was the large-scale development during the 1960s of the new practice of growing plants for sale in containers. The compost used in such containers comprised up to 100 per cent peat content – four times a much as that in the John Innes range.

Traditionally peat had been cut by hand. It is believed that the Romans were the first to dig peat out of the ground to use as fuel. Turfing took place in the summer months when the ground was driest. Entire families would be involved in cutting the peat, stacking it in turves to dry, then moving it onto peat carts to be sold locally. From the 1960s, however, major commercial companies such as Fisons introduced intensive methods of extraction that resulted in virtual opencast peat mining. The process involved massive drainage schemes, then vegetation clearance, breaking up, or scarping off, the peatland surface to allow it to dry out before mining. The 'block cutting' method Fisons introduced in the 1960s was developed into a technique of extraction using huge milling machines. By the end of the twentieth century, each year an estimated 3 million cubic yards of peat was being sold to commercial and amateur gardeners. Peat use actually increased between 1993 and 1997 by a staggering 57 per cent. It has been estimated by the Royal Botanic Gardens at Kew that over 94 per cent of the peatbogs in Great Britain had been damaged or destroyed. Most of that damage has occurred in the last fifty or so years, since the promotion of widespread use of peat for the horticultural industry. In Northern Ireland some 92 per cent of the raised bog habitat has been damaged. To cater for British gardeners' appetite for peat compost, by the start of the twenty-first century 40 per cent of peat used was being imported from Ireland. Shamrock Peat, supplied by Bord na Mona, mostly comes from central Eire – indeed, it has been one of Ireland's biggest exports.

The natural process by which peat is made is slow, allowing some moss vegetation to regenerate at an average growth rate calculated to be no more than a tenth of an inch per year. Thus when peatlands are intensively mined, rather than harvested, by such mechanical means they become a bare desert and there is virtually no chance for them to recover. Yet peatlands, mostly because of their rare animals and plants, are unique and important places for conservation. They form habitats for indigenous butterflies, moths, beetles, dragonflies and some of Britain and Ireland's rarest insects, as well as mire-dependent birds. They contain unusual plants, such as sundews, butterworts and bladderwort, which ingeniously supplement their diet in their nutrient-poor environment by catching and digesting insects. Peatbogs also help to protect the earth from global warming. As plants grow they absorb carbon dioxide, which is captured within the plant structure and stored as the plants turn to peat. When peatlands are drained or disturbed the peat starts to decompose, causing a rapid loss of stored carbon. The carbon dioxide is released back into the atmosphere, where it is a potent greenhouse gas.

Of the peatlands in existence, there are two basic types: blanket bogs, which are expansive and generally formed in wet, or upland, areas; and raised bogs, which are generally formed in smaller lowland areas. Unfortunately, it is the endangered raised bogs that are the most important scientifically. Peatbogs preserve an

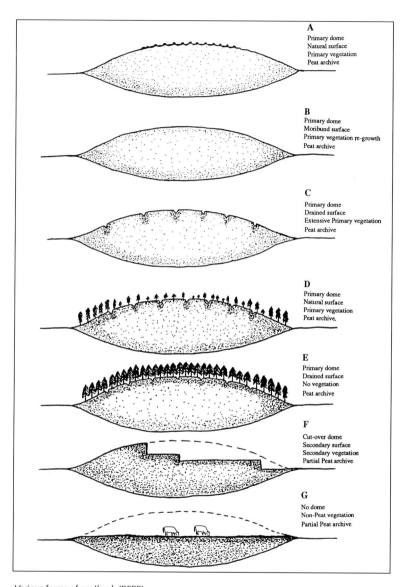

A
Primary dome
Natural surface
Primary vegetation
Peat archive

B
Primary dome
Moribund surface
Primary vegetation re-growth
Peat archive

C
Primary dome
Drained surface
Extensive Primary vegetation
Peat archive

D
Primary dome
Natural surface
Primary vegetation
Peat archive.

E
Primary dome
Drained surface
No vegetation
Peat archive

F
Cut-over dome
Secondary surface
Secondary vegetation
Partial Peat archive

G
No dome
Non-Peat vegetation
Partial Peat archive

Various forms of peatland. (RSPB)

unparalleled record of history, much of which is organic and has the capacity to expand historical understanding of peoples, cultures, the economy and climate of many centuries ago. The lowest stratas of peatbogs can be thousands of years old and have produced some of the most spectacular archaeological finds in Britain, including preserved human bodies such as that of 'Pete Marsh', the 2,300-year-old Lindow Man in Cheshire. As a result of the new awareness of the value of peatbogs came the reports *Gardening Without Peat* by Friends of the Earth in 1991 and *Out of the Mire* by Plantlife in 1992, which brought public attention to the destruction of the peatlands.

As long ago as the early 1970s various direct actions were taken by militant environmentalists against further peat extraction, most notably at Yorkshire's main raised bogs – Thorne and Hatfield Moors. Saboteurs, called 'Bunting's Beavers', dynamited dams which had been installed by Fisons' workers to drain Thorne Moors before strip-mining hundreds of acres of peat there. By the start of the twenty-first century other militant groups were making coordinated attacks against the mechanisms of extraction at peatlands in various parts of the country.

In contrast, the efforts made by more responsible environmental groups have been towards getting lowland bogs declared Areas of Special Scientific Interest (ASSI) and Special Areas of Conservation (SAC), and acquiring their own peatlands, as Plantlife have done. All the while that the fuss of recent years was going on, trials of peat alternatives were being conducted by Mike Pollock for the Royal Horticultural Society at Wisley. Using John Innes compost as the standard to set against, from 1990 various options were considered, including coconut fibre, pumice, woodfibre and leaf mould. Coconut fibre, which performed best, had been known for some time to be a fine rooting medium and soil improver, and

Hans Lenke's Golf Ball Greenhouse

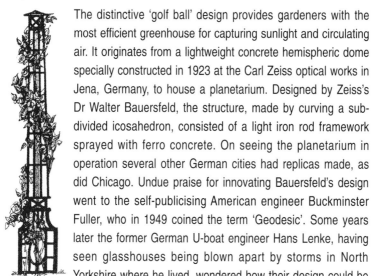

The distinctive 'golf ball' design provides gardeners with the most efficient greenhouse for capturing sunlight and circulating air. It originates from a lightweight concrete hemispheric dome specially constructed in 1923 at the Carl Zeiss optical works in Jena, Germany, to house a planetarium. Designed by Zeiss's Dr Walter Bauersfeld, the structure, made by curving a sub-divided icosahedron, consisted of a light iron rod framework sprayed with ferro concrete. On seeing the planetarium in operation several other German cities had replicas made, as did Chicago. Undue praise for innovating Bauersfeld's design went to the self-publicising American engineer Buckminster Fuller, who in 1949 coined the term 'Geodesic'. Some years later the former German U-boat engineer Hans Lenke, having seen glasshouses being blown apart by storms in North Yorkshire where he lived, wondered how their design could be improved. Lenke was so inspired by the huge 'golf ball' domes Buckminster Fuller had developed for the early-warning radar at Fylingdales, that he adopted that shape and in 1969 produced the first European 14ft domestic geodesic greenhouse.

Geodesic greenhouses were ideal for windswept gardens, such as these on the Isle of Skye in 2004. (Solardome Industries Ltd)

had been used as far back as the 1850s when inexpensive supplies were made available by firms in Bristol and Kingston-upon-Thames as a waste product from brush- and mat-making industries. Unfortunately the John Innes Horticultural Institution never considered recommending it for use in their composts. Nevertheless, the organic gardening movement has seen gardeners such as Bob Flowerdew, Geoff Hamilton and Pippa Greenwood persuade the public to think in terms of peat-free compost.

In 1945 the John Innes Horticultural Institution sold Merton Park – apparently because of poor soil there – and in 1960 moved to Hertfordshire, then to Norfolk in 1967 where it became known as the John Innes Centre. When he died in 1904 John Innes was buried in a splendid tomb in the churchyard of St Mary the Virgin, Merton Park, where four Burne-Jones windows made in stained glass were installed in his memory. On a wall of what used to be Merton Park there is a blue plaque honouring his achievement in founding the institution. The holly hedges in the suburban gardens of the nearby conservation area are a reminder of his enthusiasm for holly trees.

John Innes Centre, www.jic.ac.uk.

3

Invaders and Infiltrators

Sales by Auction.

TO GENTLEMEN, FLORISTS, AND OTHERS.

M ESSRS. PROTHEROE AND MORRIS will sell by Auction, at the Mart, Bartholomew-lane, on TUES-DAY, June 1, and THURSDAY, June 3, at 12 o'clock, a first-rate collection of Dahlias, the newest varieties of Fuchsias, Verbenas, Calceolarias, &c. ; Geraniums in bloom, with a large and rich assortment of Plants for Bedding.—May be viewed the morning of sale. Catalogues had at the Mart ; and of the Auctioneers, American Nursery, Leytonstone, Essex.

RARE AND VALUABLE ORCHIDS.
THE FIRST PORTION OF THE COLLECTION OF MESSRS. LODDIGES AND SONS.

M R. J. C. STEVENS will sell by Auction, at his Great Room, 38, King-street, Covent-garden, on TUES-DAY, June 15, at 12 for 1 o'clock, the FIRST PORTION of this celebrated Collection of ORCHIDS (which contains upwards of 2000 species) ; it will be found to comprise many fine specimens of the most rare and beautiful varieties, too numerous to mention ; the smaller plants, which are in remarkably fine health, will be lotted in a manner that will afford persons commencing the cultivation of this interesting tribe an opportunity of purchasing, which has never before o curred. — Catalogues are preparing, and will be ready a week before the sale.

LODDIGES' NURSERY.

The Entire STOCK of this Renowned Establishment, the Sale of which will extend over a period of several months. By direction of the surviving Partner of the old and respected firm of CONRAD LODDIGES and SONS, who is relinquishing the business in consequence of the lease expiring at Lady-day next.

M R. J. C. STEVENS is favoured with instructions to Sell by Auction, without any reservation, during the months of June, July, August, September, and October next, on the Premises at Hackney, and at his Great Room, 38, King-street, Covent-garden, the UNRIVALLED ASSEM-BLAGE OF EXOTIC AND OTHER PLANTS in the above-named Establishment ; more detailed particulars of which and the days of Sale will be announced in subsequent advertisements.   38, King-street, Covent-garden, May 29.

Auction advertisements featuring Loddiges's Nursery. (*Gardeners' Chronicle*, 1852)

Conrad Loddiges's Rhododendron

Adored by collectors, most rhododendrons are perceived to command a high social cachet, indeed so much so that they are unduly prevalent at prestigious events such as the Chelsea Flower Show. Conrad Loddiges, the pioneering horticulturalist who introduced the common rhododendron (*Rhododendron ponticum*) into British gardens, deserves to be a hero – although perhaps not as much as he deserves condemnation as a villain, because in certain rural parts of the British Isles Conrad's wonder plant has come to be regarded as an infuriating nuisance.

In appearance the *R. ponticum* seems innocuous enough. An evergreen with waxy deep-green tapered leaves on spreading branches, it forms dense thickets of shrub up to 15ft in height. The large blooms it produces consist of flowers with a diameter of some 3in which grow in clusters of eight to fifteen flowers. Mauve in colour, with petals spotted towards the centre, the blooms which appear in the late spring are a spectacular sight. The *R. ponticum*'s main natural distribution area as a flowering plant was the Caucasus (its name possibly derives from the Pontus region on the edge of the Black Sea). Realising there might be a market in the British Isles for such a plant, Conrad Loddiges must have assumed he was doing the right thing in importing them.

Conrad Loddiges (1738–1826) was a skilful German-born gardener whose grandfather had worked as a gardener for the Electors of Hanover – who from 1714 were kings of England.

While employed as a gardener in Velzen, near the Netherlands town of Haarlem, where there were many country houses, Conrad Loddiges apparently grew the mauve *R. ponticum* which he had obtained from the Caucasus, via Turkey, sometime earlier. At Haarlem he became professionally acquainted with the family of Sir John Silvester, an army physician. He must have made a favourable impression because in 1760 Dr Silvester, having acquired a fine house with landscaped grounds in Hackney, East London, invited Loddiges to superintend the gardens. Thus in 1761 Loddiges came to England as the Silvesters's gardener, employed to relandscape the Hackney grounds into a less formal style and to establish a variety of foreign shrubs. Loddiges brought with him from Velzen some seeds of the mauve common rhododendron, which he then planted in the army doctor's garden.

Soon showing signs of life, the seedlings became the first *R. ponticum* plants of their kind to be successfully grown in England. In 1763 Conrad became the first person to supply and market the young rhododendrons when he sold the first plant to the Marquis of Rockingham, a distinguished promoter of gardening. The timing of that accolade could scarcely have been more fortunate because, perhaps unbeknown to Loddiges, the *R. ponticum* had also been found growing in the wild in Spain, near Cadiz, and in 1763 was brought to England via Gibraltar. Not only was it astonishing that the same species should exist in two separate regions, as wide apart as Spain and the Black Sea; eventually similar seed arrived from as far afield as China.

Having in 1770 sought Dr Silvester's advice on starting a business that could make good use of his horticultural talents, Conrad struck lucky when a superb commercial opportunity arose. From Hackney an eminent Hanover-born nurseryman named John Busch was leaving for Russia to become Catherine the Great's head gardener and landscape architect. Busch had already made a good reputation for the business by obtaining seeds from all over the world through Peter Collinson, a trader in Mill Hill, and supplying exceptional plants to the private garden of Princess Augusta, at Kew. Indeed, the nursery had also become significant in the supply of seeds to German gardens. Thus Conrad's acquisition in 1771 of the Busch enterprise brought him a seed and nursery business, which he eventually relabelled with his Loddiges surname.

In 1777 Conrad published the Loddiges Nursery's first catalogue. Written in three languages – German, English and Latin – it was quite a novelty at that time and ought to have helped the sales distribution of the *R. ponticum*. In fact, initially the *R. ponticum* did not do well with the buying public: its colour was unfashionable and it was too expensive. For decades the plant sold just moderately well on the strength of its establishing a reputation for ornamental quality, although, from about 1800 onwards, it began to be widely used for under-planting woodlands on country estates. What really transformed its fortunes was the invention in 1867 of the new sporting shotgun, which made game shooting popular and led to an enthusiasm for planting heathland game cover. The *R. ponticum* became much used for that purpose because it was rabbit-proof and provided dense shelter for the sporting birds.

The Loddigeses by then were very much in the forefront of the ornamental rhododendron trade. Before the first appearance of the *R. ponticum* at Hackney in 1761, a few other rhododendrons had been brought to England, most notably the *Rhododendron hirsutum* in 1656. Nevertheless, these early introductions from

Conrad Loddiges, the well-meaning horticulturalist who introduced the nuisance common rhododendron. (Hackney Archives)

Europe and North America mostly failed, either physically, because it was not realised they required to be in acidic soil to flourish; or commercially because their colours were unappealing. The latter situation became transformed by the Loddiges Nursery's endorsement in 1833–4 of a round-the-world trip by some prototypes of Dr Nathaniel Ward's glazed 'Wardian' cases. These ingeniously simple containers invented by the East London GP, enabled seedlings to be transported thousands of miles and so revolutionised the international plant trade. Then, significantly, plant-hunting expeditions financed by the Loddigeses could reliably send to Britain hitherto unseen exotic rhododendrons. In this way Sir Joseph Hooker was able to introduce for the Loddigeses the sensationally colourful *Rhododendron thomsonii* and *Rhododendron falconeri* from the Himalayas.

Demands for these prestigious introductions flowed in from country houses. Enthusiasm also grew for the breeding of various hybrids, for which purpose Loddiges had fortunately already discovered that the sturdy *R. ponticum* made a superb root stock – indeed their 1826 catalogue, then in its fourteenth edition, listed eighteen varieties of *ponticum*. Subsequently the Loddigeses, and other breeders (most notably the Revd William Herbert, a brother of the Earl of Carnarvon of Highclere Castle), increasingly used it as a grafting varieties for less vigorous and more colourful varieties from places such as China and the Himalayas. Thereby it enabled exotic-looking rhododendrons – and also azaleas – to be widely grown for prestigious purposes in the grounds of country houses. By late Victorian times rhododendrons of all sorts had become popular evergreen shrubs. In *The Amateur's Flower Garden* (1871) Shirley Hibberd wrote that 'the money spent on rhododendrons during twenty years in this country would nearly suffice to pay off the National Debt'.

At Highclere, the first private garden to become famous for its rhododendron hybridisation programme, the *Gardener's Magazine* reported in 1834 the presence of 100 bushes of rhododendron hybrids. According to Brent Elliott, writing in *The Rhododendron Story*, Cynthia Poston (ed.), another example of such profusion was Cragside, in Northumbria, where in 1864 Lord Armstrong began transforming some 17,000 acres of bleak hillside into a thicket of coniferous and rhododendron forest. By 1892 the *Gardener's Magazine* could describe Cragside as having 'impenetrable thickets' of hundreds of thousands of bushes, 'blooming so profusely as to light up the whole hillside with their varied colours'.

The earliest signs that this wonder plant also had the potential to become problematic appeared in 1829 at Fonthill, where an abundance of self-seeded rhododendrons was found. Then, in the first volume of the *Gardener's Chronicle* (1841), Philip Frost, the head gardener at Dropmore (one of the first to use rhododendrons in a woodland setting), reported: 'In the woods here we have thousands of self-sown seedling *Rhododendrum. ponticum*, growing on any kind of soil.' The discovery of these self-seeding qualities in the 1840s meant that gardeners no longer (unless they were in a hurry) needed to purchase seedlings. This and the development of the *R. ponticum* for covert planting caused an increase in the widespread use of the plant. In the early 1860s the Covent Garden seedsman Peter Barr was selling packets of mixed seed for scattering in woodlands for a 'richly floriferous effect'. That trend was further encouraged by the publication in 1870 of William Robinson's *The Wild Garden*.

However, such was the kudos of the rhododendron, that responsible organisations who ought to have known better were slow to curb it. An early cause célèbre in that respect was Stourhead, in Wiltshire. In the 1830s virtually all its rhododendrons were *R. ponticum*. However, under National Trust ownership, they were allowed to grow unchecked around its famous lakeside (indeed, controversially, a few other rhododendrons were added as well). Unfortunately, Graham Stuart Thomas, the National Trust's influential Gardens Adviser, was an enthusiastic *R. ponticum* fan who as late as 1984 reputedly praised it for its 'supreme value in the landscape'.

When more was understood of the workings of the *R. ponticum*, it became apparent that part of the profusion was caused by wind-blown seeds. Each flower head could produce some 5,000 seeds. Thus each spring a large bush could be capable of releasing over 1 million seeds. Those seeds, said to be some of the smallest in the plant kingdom, could be dispersed by wind, in open conditions, at distances in excess of 50yd. Seeds became particularly successfully established on a thin carpet of moss. Moss carpets could be

Initially the common rhododendron seemed an ideal plant for gardens of country estates and as cover for sporting birds, but it has since overrun parts of the countryside. (Mary Evans Picture Library)

created by ground disturbance caused by overgrazing by animals, fire, scrub and forest clearance. Thus rhododendrons could spread rapidly along avenues of disturbed ground with mossy habitats, especially beneath power lines. There was much felling of woodlands during the Second World War (for example 10,640 acres of woodland in Wales were classified as devastated in 1947), which might have contributed to the spread.

Another characteristic of the plant was its ability to spread by lateral horizontal growth – its branches, on contact with the ground, being able to take root and form new plants. Over several years a single plant could cover an area of 100sq yd, reach a height of 30ft and would be capable of completely overgrowing a watercourse, thus severely affecting animal life in the stream. The neglect of country estates, because of death duties or military expediencies during the Second World War, caused many of the great rhododendron gardens to become overgrown; and thereby the plant escaped from private gardens into the open country. Such was the rhododendron's ability to spread that sometimes isolated clumps, originally planted for the purposes of game bird coverts, joined together. So dense could the rhododendron become that its heavy leaf canopy shaded much of the available light before it reached the ground, thereby inhibiting the growth of competing native plants. Also, its shallow root system exudes a chemical that acts as a weedkiller and pesticide. Few other plants survive in *R. ponticum*-dominated areas. Only the trees above the rhododendron are able to cope and as they die there may be no replacements because seeds cannot germinate and establish seedlings under the canopy.

There were few factors in *R. ponticum*'s favour beyond it reputedly providing protection for songbirds. In fact it greatly reduced the number of breeding birds in woodlands – sometimes by as much as 75 per cent. Such was its destruction of native habitats that it caused the disappearance of an estimated 150 species from Britain. As its leaves were highly toxic, it was avoided by most herbivorous livestock, leaving little to curb its spread into pastureland. Its leaf buds exuded a sticky substance that trapped most leaf-eating insects, although bees were especially fond of its rich pollen, which was unfortunate because the resulting honey is so poisonous to humans it can cause 'Mad Honey Disease'!

The ideal conditions for the common rhododendron were found to be the acidic soils in frost-free areas of high humidity on Britain's Celtic fringe. Thus it thrived in the oak woodlands of the west coast of Scotland. Unfortunately those endangered oak trees were internationally important and put the rare lichen and moss communities that were there under threat. In the Snowdonia National Park, which encompasses 10 per cent of Britain's oak woodland, the *R. ponticum* grew out of control. The common rhododendron was introduced to Northern Ireland many decades ago as cover for game and for ornamental purposes. Since then it has posed a threat to the natural vegetation of many areas of woodland in the province, where some hillsides have become overrun with dense thickets of the species. The plant had also become naturalised in Belgium and France.

The most effective means of controlling the spread of the common rhododendron was to winch out whole rootballs of bushes and burn the debris. However, bonfires cause air pollution, and so during the 1950s a variety of chainsaw, rotovating and bulldozing methods were tried in certain parts of the country. Yet some eight years later when the razed land was found to have reverted to its original state, this method was proved ineffective because of the stem fragments and reinvasion by seeds from surrounding mature bushes. In the absence of effective biological predators, chemical means have been dabbled with to control the rhododendron. The glossy waxy foliage of the plant has presented a serious obstacle to herbicide application, and means that chemical doses have to be reapplied over several years. A more efficient method, tried in western Scotland and Wales, has been to inject herbicides into the stem. All methods of control are expensive in terms of effort and cost. In Snowdonia in recent years expenditure on rhododendron eradication has been in excess of £45 million, despite the support of hordes of British Trust for Conservation Volunteers.

The good-natured Conrad Loddiges, who unintentionally began this invasion, died in 1826. Through his sons and grandchildren the Loddiges Nursery grew to become something of a pioneering horticultural institution, with the world's largest commercial collection of tropical palms and orchids. The Loddigeses were at the forefront of the fern craze in the late 1840s and 1850s, and introduced, initially in Conrad's time, hundreds of species. Unfortunately some of those ferns also escaped into the wild, infesting heathlands in south-east England: Conrad did even more damage than was originally thought.

Snowdonia National Park, www.eryri-npa.co.uk; Stourhead, Wilts, www.nationaltrust.org.uk. Some of the finest rhododendron collections are at the Royal Botanic Gardens, Kew, www.rbgkew.org.uk; and Hillier Nursery, Hants, www.hilliergardens.org.uk.

Richard Bradley's Water Plants Tub

In ancient times the Chinese, and subsequently the Japanese, grew plants such as water lilies in vases and urns. The first European known to have advocated that form of water gardening was the writer Richard Bradley. In his 1717 book *New Improvements of Planting and Gardening* Bradley advised using, in the absence of ponds or rivers:

either large Garden-Pots glazed within side, and without holes in their bottoms, or else cause some Troughs of Wood to be made, of Oaken Boards, about two Inches thick; such cases should be six Foot long, two Foot wide at the Bottom, and two Foot and a half deep, if they are for large Plants that grow under Water, or shallower for such as do not require deep water; the Corners and other Joints of such Cases, should be strengthen'd with Iron, and Insides well pitch'd and the Outsides painted.

Bradley also advised on planting techniques by which such troughs could be used to best effect. The idea of using old stone troughs and sinks to grow alpines was popularised in the 1920s by the innovative plantsman Clarence Elliot, who wrote prolifically on the subject and exhibited such containers at the Chelsea Flower Show.

In 1717 Bradley's wooden trough showed Europeans how to do simple water gardening. (Huxley, *An Illustrated History of Gardening*, Paddington Press, 1978)

Emilio Levier's Giant Hogweed

In the 1970s stories appeared in national newspapers of huge, fast-growing weeds that had suddenly appeared along the banks of Britain's rivers. Hitherto virtually unheard of, the 'giant hogweed' was a toxic plant dangerous to anyone who found it in their garden. It became the tallest herbaceous plant growing in Britain, was immortalised in a rock song and in 2003 was acknowledged by *The Guinness Book of World Records* as the largest weed in the world.

The culprit responsible for bringing the giant hogweed (*Heracleum mantegazzianum*) to Britain was Emilio Levier. The future plant collector was born in Bern in 1839, and by 1865 was known to be a doctor in Florence. He was also a botanist, and as such travelled to Spain, Portugal and then the Caucasus. In 1900 he produced with the Italian naturalist Stefano Sommier (1848–1922) *Enumeratio plantarum anno 1890 in Caucaso lectarum*, a book on the plants of the Caucasus. In Paris in 1905 another book by Emilio Levier appeared, this time heavily illustrated: *A Travers le Caucase*, also on the plantlife of the Caucasus. Seemingly while on a plant-hunting expedition in that part of the world in 1893 Levier had discovered the giant hogweed in the north Caucasus (between Russia and Turkey). In that year he reputedly sent the seeds to Kew Gardens in style – aboard the Orient Express!

Or so it would seem. Intriguingly, in 1836 John Claudius Loudon vividly described in the *Gardener's Magazine* a remarkably similar plant – which he called the 'Siberian Cow Parsnip' – growing in his garden. 'The magnificent umbelliferous plant,' he reported, 'when grown in good soil, will attain the height of upwards of 12 ft. Even in our crowded garden in Bayswater, it last year (1835) was 12 ft when it came into flower . . . Its seeds are now (July 29) ripe; and we intend to distribute them to our friends: not because the plant is useful, for we do not know any use to which it can be put.' From where Loudon obtained that quite remarkably large 'Siberian Cow Parsnip' is unclear. His description is particularly surprising because of his emphasis on the plant being 12ft tall. In fact the cow parsnip – the *Heracleum lanatum* native from the Pacific north-west to Alaska – rarely exceeds 6ft! In most other respects it is remarkably similar to the giant hogweed (*Heracleum mategazzianum*). So perhaps Loudon's wonder plant was in fact the latter. In April 1983 further doubt was caused when the *Guardian* newspaper speculated that giant hogweed had originally arrived in Britain by accident as seeds in bales of cotton from Egypt.

Nevertheless, the plant Emilio Levier did find must have seemed a magnificent sight – something like a grotesquely large carrot. Some 15ft high, it had a ribbed tubular main stalk, off which grew branches supporting enormous shiny, dark-green highly lobed leaves perhaps 40in across. At its very top was a large flat umbrella-shaped head of white flowers, which each spring could in total produce some 50,000 seeds. In fact the reason why the giant hogweed looked like a carrot (or if not a huge cow parsnip) was because it was a member of the umbelliferae family. Presumably if its natural habitat in the Caucasus was known to have been wet areas such as river-banks, marshes and woodland, at Kew it was probably planted with other exotics at the edge of the Royal Botanic Garden's main lake. There it would have been regarded as an innocuous ornamental plant distinctive for its architectural beauty. So in the 1920s there would have been no cause for alarm when the giant hogweed somehow 'escaped' – or was deliberately released – from Kew. On the strength of its

Giant hogweed: an invasive species, originally grown as an ornamental plant on country estates, before it escaped into the countryside. (CABI-Bioscience)

ornamental qualities the plant was subsequently sold by various nurseries to the public as the 'cartwheel flower'. It was purchased largely to provide structural interest in the grounds of private estates.

Emilio Levier died in 1911, perhaps quite unconcerned for the plant he had introduced to Britain. Nor, seemingly, was there reason for anyone else to be concerned until the summer of 1970 when newspaper stories appeared of giant hogweed appearing in a variety of places, including the Thames Estuary, River Mersey, Lancashire and other parts of the North of England, and particularly the north-east of Scotland. Along the banks of the

Tweed on the borders of England and Scotland it was said to be growing out of control 'like wildfire'. Elsewhere, it was seen springing up on abandoned waste ground and even in private gardens.

That summer, national newspapers outbid each other to produce the most vivid headlines: the *Daily Mail* reported 'Army routs itchy invader'; *News of the World*, 'Get Your Giant Hogweed Here'; the *Daily Telegraph*, 'Doctors worried by "escaped" Giant Hogweed'; and the *Daily Mirror*, 'The Invasion of the Giant Hogweed'. The latter went so far as to have their own special 'Doomwatch' team investigate the interloper, asking crucial questions such as: what does the giant hogweed look like? Where does it grow? How does the giant hogweed spread? To add to the sense of fun, the alien was said to be redolent of the killer plants in John Wyndham's 1951 science fiction novel *The Day of the Triffids* (which might have been inspired by the native hogweed, which only grows to some 6ft).

Matters became more serious with an article in the medical journal *The Lancet* on 3 July 1970, noting the plant 'was once a gardener's curiosity, but it is now a pest in many areas, having become more widespread in the past five years', and warning of the health risks of giant hogweed. Essentially the plant was hazardous to humans because it was phototoxic with small bristles coated with a poisonous sap on its stems and leaves. The sap consisted of phototoxic chemicals that become caustic when exposed to sunlight, sensitising the skin's natural protection against ultraviolet radiation. Direct contact with the giant hogweed could bring a rash within twenty-four hours, then severe burns and painful watery blisters that were slow to heal and in severe cases might require hospital treatment. Scarring and pigmentation of the skin could cause chronic photodermatitis, which can become recurrent and then take six years to disappear. Also the presence of minute amounts of sap in the eyes could lead to temporary, or even permanent, blindness.

The reason why the giant hogweed suddenly became a villainous plant in 1970 seems to have been because of the exceptionally hot weather Britain was suffering that summer. Why, in the fifty years or so that the plant had been in the public domain, it had hitherto failed to cause any serious problems was otherwise a mystery, and gardeners who had grown it for many years were puzzled as to why it was causing so much fuss. That summer there was a slowness to appreciate just what a wicked public nuisance giant hogweed really was. Until July one of the country's leading specialist seed companies, Thompson and Morgan, were still selling giant hogweed seeds – for 2s a packet! Several eminent gardeners were reported to be still growing it. The Bishop of Lincoln, Dr Kenneth Riches, admitted to the *Daily Express* to be deliberately cultivating the plant in his 2-acre cathedral garden, where he had even devised a simple practical means of keeping it in check: 'I stop them spreading by cutting off the seed parts before the seeds have a chance to disperse.' He claimed: 'I think the dangers are exaggerated. It is really an allergy which affects

Worst Plant Invaders

Himalayan balsam (*Impatiens glandulifera*)
Fairy fern (*Azolla filiculoides*)
New Zealand pygmy weed (*Crassula helmsii*)
Parrot's feather (*Myriophyllum aquaticum*)
Floating pennywort (*Hydrocotyle ranunculoides*)

(RHS, 2005)

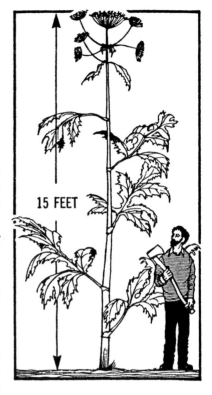

Newspapers in the early 1970s and 1980s reported horror stories about how giant hogweed could quickly grow to 15ft. (*Sunday Times*, 11 July 1982)

15 FEET

some people and not others.' At the Buckingham Palace garden parties that summer guests even noticed giant hogweed being nonchalantly allowed to flourish decoratively by the palace lake. Meanwhile, in the same year, the Royal Society for the Protection of Birds issued 40,000 copies of *The Birds in Your Garden*, a booklet advising how to establish nature reserves in gardens and advocating using giant hogweed to attract a variety of tits.

The flat seeds released by the giant hogweed could remain fertile for many years. They could be dispersed by wind, or in soil by vehicles. However, the seeds were easily transported by water, and were most commonly dispersed by plants growing on riversides being swept downstream and establishing themselves further along the river-banks. Growth was extremely rapid. When seeds were established the plant could grow from ground level to 15ft in some three months. Infestations often began as a single plant that set seed and formed a dense colony. During the summer the plant's dense foliage was effective in preventing light reaching the ground beneath it. The giant hogweed so dominated its immediate area that it stifled the growth of native grasses and vegetation and so could endanger the survival of rare or important native species of plants and their associated animal life. As a perennial, the plant died back in winter, leaving the banks without vegetation and so increasingly vulnerable to the risk of rapid soil erosion (and indeed reinvasion by fresh giant hogweed seeds from upstream, thereby allowing the plant to rapidly spread further along watercourses).

Such was the troublesome reputation Emilio Levier's originally ornamental plant established for itself that the 1981 Wildlife and Countryside Act listed giant hogweed as a species forbidden to be planted or caused to grow in the wild. Still unanswered, however, was the question of how the weed could be controlled most effectively. Following the 1970 infestation, a similarly pernicious spread of giant hogweed occurred in 1982. Control of the weed then, as twelve years earlier, was initially attempted by physical means.

This involved attempting to kill the plants by cutting them at ground level with a sharp scythe or powered trimmer. To prevent splashes of sap or fragments of plant coming into contact with the face, adequate protective clothing was required, especially a face shield, rubber boots and gloves. Cutting was least hazardous if done in the early summer while the plants were still controllable. Even so, mowing had the effect of stimulating the plant, and thus had to be done consistently every fortnight to starve the root stock. If left too late, seeds would mature (as the Bishop of Lincoln had realised). As for watercourses, the debris of cut-down dried stems and heads could float down-stream to seed.

For physical means of control to be rather more effective the plant had to be cut below ground level with a spade to ensure damage to the root stock and the crown then dug out to prevent regrowth. Alternatively the plant could be pulled out by hand in the spring when the soil was moist. The remaining roots could then be brought to the surface by ploughing – although on river-banks, where giant hogweed mostly occurred, ploughing was often not a practical option. Fortunately, cattle, sheep, pigs and goats relished the plant and could feed on it without apparent ill effects. However, such herbivorous foraging was really only effective in stifling growth, not eradicating it. All forms of physical attempt at control were labour-intensive, time-con-suming and ideally had to be applied over the entire river system. They were also unlikely to be totally effective because the plant was so durable. Even after the parent plant was apparently completely removed the seeds left behind could come to life seven or possibly fifteen years later!

The chemical research company in Surrey CABI Bioscience announced in 2003 that fungi imported from the Caucasus in Russia could help to control giant hogweed. Hitherto no means of biological control was believed to exist because the plant's toxic sap was thought to act as a feeding deterrent for most insects. Nevertheless, apparently for fear of introducing yet another harmful invasive species, officialdom would not permit widescale use of biological control. The most effective means of dealing with the plant has, since the 1970s, been reckoned to be by chemical control. The weedkiller used most frequently was glyphosate, a systemic herbicide that became available to amateur gardeners, which acted by blocking the plant's enzyme system. A selective herbicide, it was absorbed through growing leaves and stems where it was translocated throughout the plant and root network, thereby allowing treatment of the plant without damaging surrounding vegetation. Repeated doses (often over many years) would kill the plant. Application was effected by spot treatment to individual plants, or by means of knapsack sprayer in areas of dense infestation. Once the area was seemingly free from the invasive weed, native species had to be established quickly to reduce the risk of recolonisation and bankside erosion. Dense grass sward tends to discourage seed germination, while

Princess Augusta's Gardens at Kew

Probably Britain's most famous garden, Kew Gardens primarily serves a scientific purpose, unlike the Royal Horticultural Society's gardens which historically have been more concerned with domestic gardening. In 1751, Frederick Prince of Wales died at Kew from pneumonia largely because of his enthusiasm for winter gardening there, where he had a residence known as the White House. Little seems to be known of the horticultural abilities of his widow, Princess Augusta, but she continued his gardening interests at Kew, where she initiated a botanic garden of some 9 acres. Advised by Lord Bute, who wanted to create a garden containing all the plants known on earth, Augusta thus effectively initiated the Royal Botanic Gardens. In 1757–60 the architect William Chambers designed several of the garden's distinctive buildings, including the 163ft pagoda, ornate temples, and the beautifully proportioned orangery. Bute was followed as unofficial director by the famous Sir Joseph Banks, under whose direction the collections were greatly augmented, and the introduction of exotic plants was accelerated. The gardens were presented to the nation by Queen Victoria in 1840, and subsequently increased to 290 acres. In 2003 they were declared a World Heritage Site.

suitable replacement species to plant along watercourses included shrubs such as bramble, hawthorn, blackthorn and dog rose, and trees such as alder and willow.

What Emilio Levier could surely never have foreseen in 1893, when he introduced his apparently innocuous plant to Britain, was that it would eventually become immortalised in music. In 1971 the rock band Genesis recorded the song 'The Return of the Giant Hogweed'. Inspired by the infestation by the plant the previous summer, the song related the story of a horticultural hogweed brought from Russia in Victorian times, which went on to threaten the human race. Now it is sung at performances by a Genesis tribute band – appropriately named 'Hogweed'!

Thomas Brocklehurst's Squirrels

Traditionally a common sight in British gardens, native red squirrels are reckoned to have been swept to the edge of extinction by descendants of invasive North American squirrels that in 1876 were released into the wild by the Cheshire country house owner Thomas Unett Brocklehurst. In fact, the foreign squirrels were not entirely to blame for the disappearance of the reds, nor have the reds entirely been paragons of virtue in the gardening world.

Thousands of years ago the red squirrel (*Sciurus vulgaris*) was itself an invader. Fossil evidence shows that by about 10,000 BC it was already in existence in Britain, while the white squirrel (*Sciurus whitei*) was dominant in the widespread boreal conifer forests. The red then replaced the white squirrel, which became extinct. Despite being one of the last mammals to reach Britain before it became isolated from the Continent, red squirrels also settled in Ireland before its separation from the British mainland. There were some remarkable ebb and flows in the red squirrel population of the British Isles. Records from the fifteenth and sixteenth centuries show that numbers of squirrels fell in Scotland and Wales. Perhaps concern about their future was the reason the artist Hans Hoffman famously produced his watercolour picture of a red squirrel in 1578. The creatures became virtually extinct in Scotland during the eighteenth century, when coincidently Scotland was experiencing a series of exceptionally cold winters. In Ireland it was said that before the beginning of deforestation in the fourteenth century a squirrel could travel from north to south of the entire island without touching the ground. Then, following agricultural clearances, by the end of the fifteenth century there were said to be no squirrels in Ireland, a situation that held until the nineteenth century, when reintroductions began.

On the British mainland a principal cause of the squirrel decline can probably also be traced to the severe felling of trees to supply the need for timber in agriculture, war and industry (in particular as fuel for Scotland's iron-smelting furnaces). At the start of the nineteenth century replanting had begun and successful efforts were made to restock the Scottish countryside with squirrels – most notably Lady Lovat's successful campaign,

Thomas Brocklehurst's release of North American squirrels in 1876 has since endangered Britain's native red squirrels. (Macclesfield Silk Museums)

begun in 1844, to reintroduce them to northern Scotland. Jessica Holme, in her book *The Red Squirrel*, claims that at the beginning of the twentieth century red squirrels were almost universally common in the British Isles and were regularly destroyed in large numbers as forestry pests. They had become such nuisances that a Highland Squirrel Club was formed, which by 1933 had records of killing some 82,000 squirrels.

In appearance the red squirrel is surprisingly compact: covered by a distinctive chestnut coat its body has an average length of 8in, and usually weighs in total some 8–12oz. The distinctive feature, which gives the red its unmistakable appearance, is its bushy tail, adding an additional 7½in to the animal's overall length. The tail has a number of functions, ranging from serving as a signalling device, to facilitating balance when running and leaping. The red's entire body is virtually geared towards activity in trees, with long powerful legs and shorter forelegs for the purpose of jumping. Red squirrels also possess excellent eyesight, enabling them to see superbly well in dim light, and they have a wide field of vision.

The red is preponderantly a tree-dweller and for much of the year concentrates its foraging in the treetops, coming down to the ground only for food, to cross open ground and occasionally to drink open water. Its agility and light weight give it an advantage in conifer woodlands because it is able to get onto thinner branches to reach spruce and pine fir cones, shoots, catkins and seeds. Their frail structure and – contrary to popular presumption – the fact that they do not hibernate, mean they must search for a variety of food throughout the year. Of necessity, they are highly opportunistic feeders, and need to grab food whenever they can get it and cache any surplus seed for use during the rest of the year. Unfortunately they do not remember where they have buried caches and are just as likely to dig up those of another squirrel as they are to retrieve one of their own. Some caches are never retrieved and the seeds may germinate where the squirrel has buried them – much to the annoyance of some gardeners!

Female squirrels are particularly dependent on a reliable food supply for their breeding success; failure to reach a minimum body weight means they are unable to breed. Another factor in their ability to survive is their vulnerability to illness. Squirrels are susceptible to coccidiosis, a debilitating condition that is a form of inflammation caused by the gut parasite *Eimeria sciurorum*. The disease was rife among red squirrel populations at the beginning of the twentieth century.

Other than that, it has been assumed for many decades that the red squirrel lived a quite idyllic existence, not being known to have any natural predators other than birds of prey. That chirpy carefree image was reinforced by the fictional Squirrel Nutkin character devised in 1903 by the best-selling novelist Beatrix Potter (1866–1943), who illustrated her works with paintings she made of red squirrels near the garden of her home in the Lake District.

Yet the good times were about to end. The grey squirrel (*Sciurus carolinensis*) was a native of the oak and hickory forests of north-east America, its range stretching from Quebec down through New Jersey and Pennsylvania, and west to Ohio. Weighing on average 12–24oz it was significantly larger then the native British red squirrel. Unlike the reds, which preferred conifers, the grey squirrels were versatile in their habitat, and on reaching Britain thrived especially well in broadleaved woodland and in mixed woodland with broadleaved trees. They ate ten times as much food per hectare as the reds; and being willing to spend more time on or near the ground, were efficient at collecting food from all parts of the tree and its environs. By letting grey squirrels escape into the English countryside, Thomas Unett Brocklehurst became the character apparently held responsible for eventually devastating the red squirrel's ubiquitous presence in England.

The Brocklehursts were a distinguished family of Cheshire silk manufacturers whose home, since 1874, had been Henbury Hall, near Macclesfield. Of Thomas Brocklehurst himself virtually nothing is known (despite his having twice been mayor of Macclesfield and High Sheriff of Cheshire). Nor is it clear how he obtained the squirrels, and why he should have kept them. He was a great traveller and brought back many interesting objects from foreign parts, including many of the rhododendrons in the garden at Henbury, which he seemingly acquired in China. Brocklehurst purchased the Henbury estate in 1874 and set about restoring the neglected gardens there, which in 1872, under the previous owner a Mrs Masland, had been badly damaged when the dams of its ornamental lakes burst. Perhaps the squirrels had been hers? Whether by accident or design, in 1876 Brocklehurst released four squirrels from the park at Henbury Hall, from where they vanished into the Cheshire countryside and began breeding. Thomas Brocklehurst also disappeared from public view. In the autumn of 1879 he embarked on a world tour, returning in 1883 to produce a book extolling the virtues of Mexico's business opportunities! He is thought to have died in 1886.

In fact, although Brocklehurst is credited with having made the first formal release of grey squirrels into the wild, mysteriously, sightings of them were said to have been made in Britain – albeit unconfirmed – as early as 1828. That year some were claimed to have been seen in Denbighshire. Others were reported to have been observed in Montgomeryshire before 1830. Who had initially brought that apparently earlier batch to Britain is quite unclear.

Henbury Hall, Thomas Brocklehurst's country house in Cheshire, from where he released the squirrels. (Macclesfield Silk Museums)

A pair of grey squirrels shot at Highfields in Nottinghamshire in 1884 – more than 30 miles away from Henbury Hall – might have derived from Brocklehurst's original group. The second known attempt at introduction – of five grey squirrels at Bushy Park, in West London, by a Mr G.S. Page of New Jersey in 1889 – was apparently unsuccessful. Ten more squirrels, imported by

Mr Page in 1890, were released by the Duke of Bedford at Woburn Abbey, Bedfordshire, where they rapidly increased. By 1920 the squirrels of Woburn had populated an area of 1,350 square miles around the original release point. In 1902 an unnamed American was responsible for the next release, this time of 100 animals in Richmond Park, Surrey.

The most damaging effect of the grey squirrel was on the red squirrel population, which was drastically reduced by the greys' spreading of Parapoxvirus, to which they themselves were immune. A deadly disease to red squirrels, Parapoxvirus was known as 'squirrel pox'. Infection resulted in symptoms not unlike those of myxamatosis in rabbits, with severe swelling around the face, and finally death. The reds are especially vulnerable to disease when they are undernourished and in poor condition. It is also possible that squirrel pox is an anxiety related disease that only emerges in red squirrel populations already suffering from food shortages or overcrowding.

What at first prompted officialdom to take action against grey squirrels was more the perceived need to protect commercial forestry than a concern to save the reds. A characteristic sign of the grey squirrel's presence is its nesting drey. Usually built in the fork of a tree some 18–49ft from the ground, it is an untidy looking nest of bark and twigs lined with grass, leaves or moss. To construct it the squirrel strips bark from trees. Outer bark is torn off for reasons of food gathering to reach the unlignified substance underneath. Infinitely more damage is done during the breeding season when frustrated male squirrels habitually vandalise bark anywhere on the main stem and branches, then mark the tree as their domain with a foul urine smell. Ring-barked trees are often killed outright, if not later by ensuing disease. Particularly vulnerable to the ripping off of their protective bark are 15- to 40-year-old hardwood trees, especially sycamore and beech. Even if the trees survive attacks, their timber quality is severely reduced. It is principally for this reason that in 1937 the importation and keeping of grey squirrels was made illegal. However, although in the 1940s and 1950s agricultural committees handed out free cartridges to squirrel-shooting clubs and paid a bounty for every squirrel killed, there is no visible impact on the grey squirrel population.

When squirrel damage leads to a loss of species, such as the beech, within woodlands, a knock-on effect can be a loss of associated fungal and invertebrate fauna and their predators. Squirrels also prey on woodland bird populations, and, for already endangered native creatures such as the common dormouse, additionally provide undue competition for food. In gardens, too, squirrels are a pest – so much so that they are perceived as 'garden rats'. If they venture into lofts of houses they can sometimes build their nesting dreys there, noisily running about and chewing through electric cables, thereby becoming a fire hazard. If cornered they can viciously attack pets and humans. Outside, they will dig holes in lawns, bury their nuts in flowerbeds, dig out bulbs, strip bark from garden trees and steal food from bird tables. Yet to non-gardeners the grey squirrel is often an entertaining sight in woodlands, parks and streets; and the television-viewing public have enjoyed programmes showing them collecting nuts by performing initiative tests. When in 2003 BBC2's *Wild in Your Garden* initiated an audience response poll to the question 'Are grey squirrels a pest?', as many as 49 per cent voted 'No'.

Such has been the increase in the grey squirrel population since 1876 that they are now said to number more than 2 million – which outstrips the native reds squirrels by sixty-six to one. In most parts of the country the reds are practically extinct and only surviving in natural havens where the interlopers cannot get at them – the Isle of Wight, islands in Poole harbour, Cumbria, Northumberland and certain isolated parts of Scotland. In January 2006 a government-endorsed national cull was announced to try to halt the declining numbers of the endangered native red population. Of rather more concern to the grey squirrels should be the reported sightings near Woburn Abbey of released so-called albino black squirrels, which are even more aggressive than the grey squirrels who have caused the reds to become virtually extinct.

Most Distinctive Carnivorous Plants

Name	Trap Resemblance
Cape sundew	Flypaper
Cobra lily	Pitfall
Genlisea	Lobster trap
Utricularia	Mousetrap
Venus fly trap	Steel trap

Philipp von Siebold's Japanese Knotweed

The most pernicious weed in Britain, Japanese knotweed far outperforms other invasive species in terms of damage done. This is all the more surprising because it looks pleasant enough. Growing in clumps to a height of some 9ft it has large oval green leaves 4¾in long and a hollow stem similar to bamboo. In early spring the plant produces fleshy red-tinged roots, and towards the end of August clusters of creamy flowers appear, which attract bees and wasps. A native to Japan, Korea, Taiwan and northern China, the natural habitat of *Fallopia japonica* is volcanic fumaroles where soil conditions are extreme or the sides of mountain streams. In southern Taiwan it grows at altitudes between 7,800 and 12,500ft; and in Japan, where it is better known, it can be found at about 7,800ft on Mount Fuji. In addition to the competition with other plants in Japan – where it is just one member of the giant herb community, all struggling for survival – the *F. japonica* is subject to predation from a whole range of invertebrates and fungi.

The character apparently most responsible for introducing the knotweed to Britain in 1850 was Philipp von Siebold (1796–1866). A Bavarian-born doctor who became a physician to King William I of the Netherlands, in 1823 he joined the Dutch East India Company, who sent him to Nagasaki. Here he restocked a medicinal garden, lectured in medicine and developed an interest in all aspects of Japan, especially the flora. He collected over 1,000 botanical specimens and illegally obtained maps of the country, but before his return to Bavaria in 1828 was arrested on charges of espionage, tried and banished for life. Nevertheless, his grateful students helped him to send 12,000 herbarium specimens to Europe, including 1,200 living specimens, although only 260 survived his return journey to the Netherlands, and then Ghent in 1830. Civil disturbance during the Belgian struggle for independence forced him to flee the city, and in the interim his plants were confiscated and redistributed among the city's nurserymen: it is not clear whether the *F. japonica* was among these. However, when peace was restored

Philipp von Seibold established a Jardin d'Acclimatization at Leiden, which he soon commercialised into the firm of Siebold and Co. Receiving a steady flow of plants from the correspondents he had established over the years he was then able to introduce Japanese varieties of many plants. Seibold wrote *Fauna Japonica*, a large illustrated flora of Japan, then in 1845 a thick *Catalogus librorum Japonicum*, which named the eventually infamous giant knotweed *Polygonum cuspidatum*.

From Siebold's nursery at Leiden the plant arrived at the Royal Botanical Gardens at Kew in August 1850 in an unsolicited parcel of plants. Then, in 1854, the plant (this time under the pseudonym *Polygonum sieboldii*) was sent to the Royal Botanic Gardens in Edinburgh. Apparently helped by the publicity provided by Siebold's written work of 1850, the plants were sold by a large number of commercial nursery gardens around the country. Seemingly an ideal ornamental plant, it was an immediate favourite with gardeners. Its dense sheaves of canes, heavy leaves and tiny white flowers suited the Victorians' austere taste. It was recommended for naturalising in the shrubbery by none other than the nineteenth-century pioneer of 'wild gardening', William Robinson, who in *The Wild Garden* (1870) described it as 'most effective in flower in the autumn' and advocated planting it in groups of two or three.

Controversy concerning the Japanese knotweed in Britain first took the form of doubts about its origins. In 1901 the Japanese botanist Makino noticed that the *Polygonum cuspidatum* introduced by Siebold was remarkably similar to a plant named *Reynoutria japonica* by Martin Houttuyn in 1777. A Dutch naturalist, Houttuyn (1720–94) had that year produced a book with the first ever illustration in the West of the Japanese knotweed. In the confusion it seems that as early as 1825 the Horticultural Society

The first illustration of Japanese knotweed available in Europe appeared in 1777. (Martin Houttuyn, *Pflazensystem nach der dreyzehnten lateinischen*, Nuremberg, 1777)

had been growing a Chinese accession of the plant in an artificial swamp in their garden in Chiswick, which was coincidentally only 3 miles east of Kew. Makino found an article in the French journal *Revue Horticole* (1858) claiming that the Japanese knotweed 'has been cultivated for twenty years in the garden of the Horticultural Society of London'. The Japanese knotweed never flowered at Chiswick, so when Makino's 1901 observations established the name *Fallopia japonica* the credit for its first introduction into England remained Philipp von Siebold's. The plant even acquired some innocuous colloquial names such as 'Japweed', 'Sally rhubarb' and 'Donkey rhubarb'.

The earliest sign that the giant knotweed had the ability to escape beyond the simple confines of horticultural experiment and become naturalised appeared in 1886 when it was seen growing on South Wales coal tips. Its invasive nature was noted in the *Journal of the Royal Horticultural Society* of 1905, which advised no further planting unless it was 'most carefully kept in check'. In the 1907 edition of *The English Flower Garden* William Robinson, who only a few years earlier had been advocating use of knotweed, was now cautioning that it was 'easier to plant than to get rid of in the garden'. In London it was first noticed in the wild in 1900; it had reached a rubbish-tip in Langley two years later; it was found near Exeter in 1908; Suffolk by 1924; West Yorkshire in the 1940s; and Northumberland in the 1950s. Abroad, too, it became conspicuous in several other European countries and especially North America, where it was observed from Louisiana in the east to central California in the west, and as far north as Alaska. It was a particular nuisance in the eastern states, where it spread along banks of rivers and also grew in wetlands.

What made the Japanese knotweed particularly problematic was the method of its dispersal and dissemination. One of the plant's most visual characteristics was its masses of white seed-producing flowers which appeared during the summer on stems that grew to a height of 6–9ft. Being deciduous, the plant's foliage died back with the first winter frost. Although during winter its green stems speckled with purple could persist as upright hollow stalks, there was an apparently innocuous, though unsightly, mass of tangled dead vegetation. Then, in the spring, fleshy red shoots appeared. The white seeds were, in fact, rarely responsible for the Japanese knotweed's progress over ground – much of its expansion was achieved by phenomenal vegetative growth from the roots. The vigorous red shoots that appeared at ground level could grow at an astonishing speed of almost an inch every twenty-four hours.

It is a plant that can fully reproduce itself, forming a new plant from a root (rhizome) fragment of only ⅖in. These fragments can be created by mechanical flails and mowers, then unwittingly dispersed locally on derelict land or by simply dumping garden waste. Movement of rhizome fragments downstream within river systems and movement of contaminated soil became significant means by which new sites were established. The plant also has the potential to be spread by sea, though it is more likely to take root beside inland water (ditches, streams, canals, lakes), beside linear terrestrial features (roads, paths, hedges, embankments), or on the edges of semi-natural vegetation (woodlands, sand dunes).

In recent years Japanese knotweed has become a serious nuisance, causing damage especially to disturbed land associated with paths, roads, car parks, buildings and along watercourses. Often a principal cause of damage has been the plant's roots, which can extend 21ft outwards and reach 6ft deep. So dense can be the root network below ground that it forms a heavy woody mass weighing some 50lb per cubic yard. Unfortunately, not only can the knotweed spread rapidly (in a year one plant can cover the area of a tennis court), it can also do considerable structural damage on its journeys below ground, sometimes forcing shoots between concrete pavements and walls. Damage can also be done to herbaceous species and young woody plants, which are overrun and excluded by this aggressive weed. Once established, Japanese knotweed shades out other plants by producing a dense canopy of leaves early in the growing season. The tall growth can be visually obtrusive and block sight lines along roads, paths and rivers. By damaging river-banks it can increase the risk of flooding. And, while providing a harbour for vermin, the plant only offers a poor habitat for native insects, birds and mammals.

Alarmed at the spread of Japanese knotweed, in 1981 Parliament agreed to a clause in the Wildlife and Countryside Act making it an offence to knowingly 'plant or otherwise encourage' the growth of Japanese knotweed in the countryside – which could be done by cutting the plant or roots and disturbing surrounding soil. A measure of the seriousness of the knotweed threat is the fact that the only other land plants so banned by name in the 1981 legislation was giant hogweed. By then

Japanese knotweed was brought to Britain in 1845, via Europe, where enthusiasm for oriental plants was stimulated by Philipp von Siebold's books, such as *Flora Japonica*. (Philipp von Siebold, *Flora Japonica*, Lugduni Batavorum, 1835)

knotweed had become one of the worst conservation problems in western Britain and in major conurbations in England and Wales. In some localities infestations were virtually impossible to control and continued to spread rapidly, sometimes covering areas so densely that they became pure monocultures of knotweed.

The most direct means of controlling the infestations of the plant unwittingly introduced numerous decades earlier by Philipp von Siebold, was to use physical force. Regular cutting with a hand scythe or pulling could produce a grass sward and slow down the encroachment of Japanese knotweed and could, after ten or more years, possibly exhaust the rhizome and kill the plant. But a knotweed stand will re-emerge if such methods are not continued because they do not entirely eradicate the weed. Also, mowing could be expensive and even impractical on steep sites or rough terrain. As the roots and rhizomes of Japanese knotweed can extend very deep in the ground, to excavate them in an untreated state is unwise – and expensive. There are also strict controls on the disposal of contaminated soil. Any excavated soil removed from areas where Japanese knotweed has established must be disposed of at a suitably licensed landfill site, buried to a depth of at least 15ft (if not 30ft) deep.

Herbicides offered the most effective methods available of controlling the knotweed. The best such chemical for that purpose was glyphosate, which first appeared in 1971. Claimed by Monsanto, its principal manufacturer, to be the world's biggest-selling herbicide, it is commonly marketed as 'Round Up'. Effective though it is on Japanese knotweed it does not affect the plant immediately. Instead, the herbicide soaks through the leaves and stalk tissue, and keeps the plant alive while the chemical travels from one cell to another in the plant's root system before apparently killing it. Even then, however, the rhizome network might still be alive. Treatment with the herbicide alone can take three years and is unlikely to completely eradicate the plant; even though it might appear to be dead, it might in fact only be dormant.

In 2003 the British Government's Non-Native Species Policy Review estimated the costs of controlling knotweed countrywide to be £1.56 billion. Although such a figure was not to be forthcoming, it provided an indication of the extent of the problem and the high costs associated with control were it to be attempted. A method that has been experimented with, though not yet released outside a laboratory, is biological control. The firm Cabi-bioscience have experimented with a fungus distributed by beetles which does have some effect against the Japanese knotweed. However, fears that these new alien species could themselves become invasive has curbed official enthusiasm for such biological remedies. Another option, and surprisingly low-tech, is to allow horses, sheep and goats to eat the shoots as fodder and thus keep the knotweed plants in check.

Fearsome though the Japanese knotweed is, it does also have certain advantages. It has been used to stabilise sand dunes and mine spoil, particularly in the United States, while in China and Korea it has been widely made into a medicine for a variety of illnesses. It can also be used for making paper; its stems form the basis of a vegetable dye; and its flowers are a source of nectar for insects such as honeybees. In Japan the knotweed is even regarded as a stir-fried delicacy. Quite independently, people in Wales have been making good use of the knotweed's culinary virtues – in parts of Dyfed the shoots and leaves are cooked like spinach. So perhaps Philipp von Siebold, the Bavarian doctor, did not necessarily do the wrong thing by importing the demon knotweed.

Most Awe-inspiring Plantage

Plant	Specification	Location
Deepest fig root	393ft	Transvaal, South Africa
Longest vine	114ft	Hampton Court, England
Tallest tomato plant	65ft	Lancashire, England
Heaviest palm seed	44lb	Praslin, Seychelles
Oldest creosote plant	11,700 years	Mojave Desert, USA

Christine Buisman and Dutch Elm Disease

Dutch elm disease is one of the world's most devastating tree afflictions. During the twentieth century, by causing the deaths of millions of elms, it ravished the appearance of countless gardens and parklands in Britain, Europe and North America. The unlikely heroine who made great efforts in 1929 to understand the composition of the disease, was a scientist from the Netherlands called Christine Buisman.

Elms were for centuries represented in Britain by many species, whose numerous hybrids made identification very difficult (unlike ash and beech which had only one species). Of the various elm types the most widespread was the common elm (sometimes known as the 'English elm'), which characteristically had a tall sturdy stem and horizontal boughs with heavy masses of foliage. Distinctively, all elm leaves were slightly uneven and double-toothed around the edges. Elm was similar in form and structure to lime, but advantageously was more easily propagated and held its leaves later in the autumn. Not only was the elm a rapid grower (some 3ft per year), it could last to a great age and was of sturdy appearance.

Such robust ornamental qualities endeared the elm to the seventeenth century's leading landscape designers. John Evelyn, noting the elm's ability to be transplanted, advised in his forestry discourse *Sylva*, 'this is an excellent and expeditious way for great persons to plant the accesses of their houses with'. Accordingly, great avenues of elm were laid out on country estates such as Blenheim and Windsor Great Park. The latter was perhaps the grandest example of all, with the original long walk planted in 1670 and the avenue running for 2 miles from the castle towards a hilltop statue. At Broughton House, in Northamptonshire, elm avenues extending over 70 miles were planted. Another great elm avenue was that in Kensington Gardens, London. In his *Remarks on Forest Scenery* Gilpin placed the elm next to the oak in its picturesque effect, and in 1791 applauded the effects of planting elms and firs alternately in the 'skreen' – the planting that divides private estates from the road. Elm became so widely planted in parklands that in John Claudius Loudon's 1838 *Arboretum et Fruicetum Britannicum* it was referred to as the second most common tree after oak in parks and pleasure grounds. Thomas Fairchild's *The City Gardener* (1737) noted how the elm was surprisingly tolerant of pollution, being able to survive in cities such as smog-polluted London. Brian Clouston claims, in *After the Elm*, that thousands of elms were planted in the capital's private gardens and in other major cities. They were also planted extensively in coastal areas because of their tolerance of salt-laden winds.

Dutch elm disease first made an appearance on elm trees in northern France in 1918. The symptoms were sudden yellowing, then browning and shrivelling of the foliage of part or all of the tree in the summer. Sometimes there was an appearance of scorching. Affected branches began to die back from the tip, then the entire tree would die back to ground level. In severe attacks the tree might be killed before the end of the summer, but even if it survived that it would die the following spring. Initially the disease was colloquially known as 'elm death' or 'elm disease'. However, as the Dutch alone were organised in their attempt to understand what it really was, by the time it was established in England it had become known as 'Dutch elm disease'.

The disease quickly spread across huge areas of north-west Europe. It appeared in Belgium and Holland in 1919, then Germany in 1921. Holland was particularly vulnerable to the epidemic because elms had been planted extensively in that country around farms and along roads in villages, towns, and along rural roads – especially near the coast, where they were one of the few trees that could survive the harsh environmental conditions created by high winds and salt. Furthermore, the vast majority of elms planted in Holland belonged to one clone, 'Belgica', which had been selected centuries earlier by Dutch nurserymen but which was highly susceptible to the disease. In Holland alone it was estimated that more than 50 per cent of the elms had been killed by 1939. The disease crossed the Alps into northern Italy in the late 1920s. There it had a particularly sweeping impact, for in addition to their growing in forests and their ornamental value, elms were used extensively for shade, shelter, and grapevine support in vineyards. The disease was transported to the United States in 1930, probably in elm burl logs shipped to Ohio to make furniture veneers. Particularly susceptible was the stately American elm, sometimes referred to as 'Nature's noblest vegetable', once a dominant forest tree as well as the most commonly planted tree in cities. From the 1930s onwards, the

Millions of elms were devastated by Dutch elm disease in the 1920s and 1970s. (Stanley Badmin and Peter Collins, *Trees of Britain, Sunday Times*, 1960)

disease caused major epidemics across much of North America, destroying some 40 million elms.

In 1927 the disease was first recorded as reaching Britain when it was sighted on a golf course in Totteridge, Hertfordshire. It began spreading across England, generally south of a line from Chester to Hull, ruining and threatening the famous elm avenues and ornamental garden trees. On 11 November 1930 it provoked an article headlined 'Stricken Elms' in *The Times*. 'No one can view with anything but concern the prospective death or maiming of the magnificent specimens of one kind of elm or another to be found on estates up and down the land.' It was calculated that there were 23 million elms in Britain in 1805: by 1937 some 10–20 per cent of these were reckoned to have been destroyed. This in turn was harmful to wildlife, because each elm had provided a home to a rich variety of butterflies, moths, beetles, lichens, mosses and fungi.

What made the sudden demise of these trees so difficult to comprehend was their reputation for sturdiness. Traditionally regarded as extremely tough and difficult to split – because of its irregular close grain – elm wood was much used for the axels of waggons and lining the floors of carts and wheelbarrows. When steamed it kept its shape. Elm was made into water pipes, lock gates and waterwheel paddles because in waterlogged conditions it was virtually indestructible. Why then did the trees so quickly fall victim to the disease?

One of the world's earliest scientific centres devoted wholly to studying plant diseases was the Willie Commelin Scholten Laboratory (WCS), which had been founded in Amsterdam in 1895 and then subsequently moved to Baarn in the central Netherlands. There, in 1920, the researcher Marie Beatrice Schwarz performed a series of tests which, by extracting microbes from diseased elms and inoculating healthy elms, indicated that a hitherto unknown fungus was causing the new disease. Unfortunately no one would believe her! Since the disease's initial appearance in 1918 tree specialists in various countries had been unable to agree what might be the cause. In France some believed it was a consequence of wartime gas poisoning; in Germany, that it might be bacterium infecting the soil; and from Belgium came the idea that it was a type of canker disease. As for Schwartz, she soon moved to the Dutch East Indies to work and get married, and her findings were forgotten.

It was not until 1929 that Dr Christine Johanna Buisman, a young researcher who had just completed a doctoral thesis on the root rot of calla lilies, was directed at the WCS to do a detailed study of the cause of Dutch elm disease. Buisman found that Schwarz's critics had been unable to reproduce the fungus because the period when elms were responsive to artificial inoculation was limited to only six weeks each summer and at that only if they were well-established trees. By successfully creating those growing conditions Christine Buisman was able to confirm the disease was caused by a yeast-like fungus (*Ophiostoma ulmi*) that clogged the elm's vascular system of arteries, preventing the vital flow of water and nutrients between the leaves and roots until the tree perished. The fungus could move from tree to tree through the root systems. Elms were especially vulnerable to disease transmission by that means because they naturally grew gregariously and were also in close proximity when formally arranged in avenues. It was apparently not until 1935 that J.J. Fransen, a scientist at Wageningen, produced a dissertation establishing that the DED fungus could also be carried by two types of elm bark beetle, the small elm bark beetle (some ⅛in long) and the large elm bark beetle (¼in long). The boreholes made by these tiny bristled

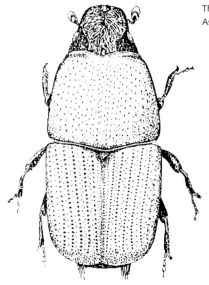

The Dutch elm beetle. (Arboricultural Association)

creatures enabled the disease to establish itself in the elms, and the yeast-like fungus the trees secreted on the beetles was carried on to other elms.

The logic of Christine Buisman's findings was that the infected trees had to be destroyed. That was because each dead tree could be open to invasion for nearly two years as a breeding ground for some 250,000 to 1 million beetle larvae which, when mature in the springtime, could spread the disease by flying from infected elms to feed in the crowns of healthy trees even several miles distant. For gardeners the elms became dangerous because of their progressive physical disintegration, making them liable to drop branches without warning and then fall over completely. So the standard method of slowing the advance of Dutch elm came to be the felling and total burning of all infected parts of the trees. By

1937 the epidemic had effectively run its course in Britain, although as late as 1954 there was apparently a last outbreak of the disease in Kensington Gardens, which led to the destruction of 200 magnificent elms there. In 1960 Dr Tom Peace, a Forestry Commission expert who had been monitoring the spread of the disease since the 1920s, optimistically prophesied: 'unless it completely changes its present trend of behaviour [it] will never bring about the disaster once considered imminent'.

All was quiet in the western hemisphere until the 1960s, when, unexpectedly, the tide of international destruction turned completely. This time its epicentre was North America, where Dutch elm had somehow developed into a new and highly aggressive fungus. Unlike the waxy yeast-like appearance of the earlier slow-growing non-aggressive strain, the new culture (*Ceratocystis ulmi*) grew fast and had a fluffy appearance. In Britain such became officialdom's complacency that the elementary quarantine precautions to prevent the spread – of importing only de-barked elm logs – were not taken. From Ontario, Canada, it reached Britain in 1965 in a cargo of unsawn elm destined for the boat-building industry (although this was not recognised as being the means of entry until 1973). The new disease first became apparent almost simultaneously in Gloucester-shire and Essex before spreading to other countries. Unfortunately, because the bark beetles thrived in hot weather, during the parched dry summers of 1975 and 1976, many more million elms became infected. No longer regarded as one of the most common trees in the country, the elm, predicted the *Daily Mail* on 8 August 1975, was 'now virtually doomed to extinction'. Because it was widely found as a hedgerow tree, in every badly affected area its demise was changing the face of the landscape. However, the encouraging of woodpeckers, and even the importing of

Austrian parasitic wasps who also were natural predators of the beetles, did nothing to help tip the balance. Some 25 million of the UK's 30 million adult elms perished in the outbreak. The only area that remained safe for old elms was Brighton and Hove – because the beetles had been unable to fly across the South Downs. A nationwide search for native English elms in 2005 found only 200 survivors.

A means to pre-empt such epidemics had been explored by Christine Buisman as early as 1929. Having confirmed what the causes of Dutch elm were, she then energetically instigated a far-reaching programme to find a disease resistance in all elms and then build on that by breeding. She travelled as a consultant to Italy, followed by a year at the Arboretum of Harvard University to advise on disease-resistant elms. Unfortunately, she never lived to see the results since she died in 1935. Other scientists continued her work – with mixed results. In America the Princeton elm, a cultivar originally selected in the 1920s for its landscape quality, has since been realised to have a considerable resistance to the disease. In the Netherlands various sturdy clones were devised and named in honour of the pioneering work done at Baarn in the 1920s, including 'Commelin', 'Bea Schwarz' and 'Christine Buisman'. In 1979 the Pitney Bowes organisation launched an 'Elms Across Europe' movement to replace elms lost by the disease. Appropriately, on the Continent and in Britain, the most widely chosen new elm was the 'Christine Buisman'.

The University of Sussex, Brighton, has a unique collection of surviving elms, www.sussex.ac.uk.

Bridges Adams' Rooftop Terrace

The first advocacy of using outside living space as an extension of British homes was made by the *Gardener's Magazine* in 1838, which suggested how lofts might be turned into greenhouses by means of forming glass windows in roofs and training vines and creepers under the roof beams. The idea was in 1859 developed further by William Bridges Adams (an engineer who had invented the system of fastening railway tracks with fishplates). In 'How to Convert London into a Garden', an article Bridges Adams penned for the journal *Once a Week*, he proposed transplanting much of the capital city's domestic life from the parlour to the rooftop garden, where housewives could relax with their families in the sunshine.

Bridges Adams urged Londoners to create rooftop gardens. (*Once a Week*, 17 December 1859)

4

Of Greatest
Advantage

A section of vineyard on a hillside. (Speechly, *Treatise on the Culture of the Vine*, Longman, 1811)

John Rose's English Vines

The recent series of exceptionally hot summers in Britain has been accompanied by discernible rises in the quality and availability of English wines. Until just a few years ago the very mention of the term English wine could invariably be guaranteed to produce a reaction redolent of a music hall joke. In fact, the story of how English wines have since Roman times struggled to develop has had some remarkable episodes. Of the various knowledgeable enthusiasts who have insisted that vines could be successfully grown in Britain, none has been more influential than the skilful seventeenth-century horticulturalist John Rose, with his book *The English Vineyard Vindicated.*

Vines were first introduced to Britain by the Romans, probably to ensure a sustained supply of wine rather than rely on an erratic seaborne supply from Italy, and their existence has been adequately confirmed by archaeological evidence. Many Roman towns in Britain, and some of the great Roman villas in Somerset and Gloucestershire, had their own vineyards, probably planted with the Pinot Noir vine. However, when the Romans eventually left, the country was plunged into the so-called Dark Ages, and warring tribes destroyed the limited civilisation that the Romans had established during their 300 years of occupation. Vine-growing was revived by the arrival of the Normans, who brought their skills in this craft with them, and within twenty years established some forty vineyards in southern Britain, some as far north as Lincoln.

Henry II's marriage to Eleanor of Aquitaine in 1154 brought all the Bordeaux winelands under English rule, with the result that the homegrown product was remorselessly ousted by the fine full-bodied Bordeaux wines. The Black Death, which devastated England in 1348, so reduced the labouring population that many vineyards were abandoned and never revived. Also, it is believed that in about 1350 the Gulf Stream changed course and the 300-year-long spell of warm weather came to an end. The Pinot Noir evidently found the cooler summers not to its liking, and the grapes failed to ripen. Many of the Norman vineyards had belonged to monasteries, and so their dissolution in 1535, and then sacking by Henry VIII's henchmen, virtually ceased widespread wine-growing in England.

Because of his track record in growing exotic plants, the famous John Rose ought to have been the right person to have revived vine-growing. Surprisingly little is known of Rose's early life. The guesstimates for his year of birth range from 1619 to 1629, although it is certain he was the younger son of a yeoman farmer from Amesbury, in Wiltshire, and that he started working life as a gardener at Amesbury House, the property of Sir William Seymour, who later became the 2nd Duke of Somerset. Rose was next made an assistant gardener at Essex House in the Strand, and in the early 1640s was sent by the Earl, its owner (a relative of the Duke of Somerset), to study under Le Notre, the great French gardener then working at Versailles. On his return Rose was appointed 'Keeper of the Garden of Essex House, Strand', a position he relinquished in 1661 on being appointed by the newly restored Charles II as the royal gardener at St James's. This promotion meant he became the person in charge of the royal

John Rose was King Charles II's gardener, and accomplished at
growing exotic fruit and vines. (Royal Botanic Gardens, Kew)

garden between the Mall and Pall Mall and, moreover, was responsible for establishing a garden and greenhouse at St James's Park.

A key factor in Rose's rapidly progressing career was his extraordinarily innate aptitude for growing almost anything. Between 1655 and 1661 he became a raiser of new varieties of auricula. He also proved to be a fine producer of 'greens', as evergreen plants were then called. According to John Rae's description of his method of cultivating them, 'These are the rules observed by Mr. John Rose, the ingenious Keeper of the Garden at Essex House in the Strand, where is now to be seen under his regiment a most noble Collection of the choicest Green and rarest shrubs that are planted in cases, in a most healthy and flourishing condition.' At the St James's garden Rose successfully planted dwarf fruit trees. The pears that he grew there, apparently on French dwarfing stocks, were widely acclaimed. In 1661 he won enormous prestige by reputedly growing the first ever pineapple raised in England. This was considered to be such a skilled accomplishment that, in August 1668, the artist Hendrick Danckerts produced an oil painting of Rose presenting Charles II with the pineapple. The more accomplished Rose became as a techno wizard who pushed plant-growing to the limit, the greater became his enthusiasm for pioneering the growing of seemingly impossible plants.

Perhaps it was a combination of enthusiasm and what he had learnt and seen of vine-growing in France, that persuaded him to write a book campaigning for a revival of vine-growing in England. The idea had evidently been buzzing about in his head as early as 1660, because sometime between October 1660 and October 1661 he happened to discuss the subject with the celebrated diarist John Evelyn at Essex House. Evelyn later recalled how when 'refreshing myself in the Garden at Essex House, and falling into discourse with Mr. Rose about Vines, and particularly the cause of the neglect of Vineyards of late England; he reason'd so pertinently upon the subject'.

The result was *The English Vineyard Vindicated* (1666), a slim leather-bound unillustrated book which was run off by John Crook at St Paul's Churchyard. Rose tackled the subject succinctly in just forty-nine pages. He wrote: 'I persuade myself it is not altogether from the defect of the climate, at least not in all places alike; nor, I am sure, of the Industry of Your Majesties' subjects.' Tactfully avoiding any sign of pouring scorn on those who did not grow vines, he adroitly set about explaining how it ought best be done: 'Gentlemen shall be encourag'd to plant these sorts of vines which I have here recommended, and to cultivate them by my directions, that precious liquor may haply againe recover its just estimation.'

According to Rose it was a myth that vines needed healthy soil. Vines, he insisted, would flourish on many patches of stony or chalky ground in southern England. In terms of preparing the ground for plantation, adding charcoal would do. He named several forms of vines, and what grapes did best in the English climate. These included the black grape (which the Romans had reputedly used), and what he called White Mufcadine, Parfly grape, Mufcadella (white grape), Frontiniaque (white and red), and Mufcadine (which he personally grew at St James's). Rose also advised how to plant, prune and govern the plantation, order and cultivate the vineyard after the first four years, when to manure with compost (lime and dung), and how to make and purify wine.

A treasure trove of sound practical advice though *The English Vineyard Vindicated* was, the book's chances of being reissued were

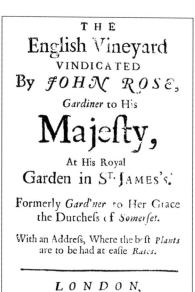

In 1666 John Rose's *The English Vineyard Vindicated* insisted that vines could be successfully grown in England. (Rose, *The English Vineyard Vindicated*, Herb Grower, 1965)

threatened in 1666 when its printers were disastrously burnt to the ground in the Great Fire of London. Serendipitously it then emerged that Rose was not the only writer of *The English Vineyard Vindicated*. Perhaps because he did not consider himself to be an author, Rose had earlier decided to allow the book to be partly ghostwritten by the accomplished writer John Evelyn, who signed the preface with the pseudonym 'Philocepos'. From the 1650s, following unsuccessful attempts to complete the ambitious *Elysium Britannicum*, the first encyclopaedia of British gardening, Evelyn had resorted to publishing sections of it separately. The most authoritative of those became *Sylva*, a discourse on forest trees, then *Pomona*, a work on cider-making and fruit trees. A wealthy amateur garden designer, Evelyn had a sound reputation for creating gardens in the French style, such as his own Sayes Court, in Deptford. Evelyn's riverside house was later leased to Peter the Great, who famously studied shipbuilding in the dockyard nearby, and at wild parties would throw bottles into the Thames – although it is not known whether they were bottles of wine!

When *The English Vineyard Vindicated* next appeared in 1669 it was bound as part of an engraved reprint of Evelyn's *The French Gardiner*, a French work on fruit tree cultivation by Nicolas de Bonnefons, which Evelyn had translated. Evelyn's endorsement of Rose's campaign to defend the quality of English vintages compared with those of the Continent began to encourage others to produce similar works. Soon *The Complete Vineyard* by William Hughes appeared, with information on the planting of vines, the gathering of grapes and on the making of wine according to methods practised in Germany and France. Hughes insisted there could be 'such vineyards and wall vines as produce a great store of excellent good wine' in spite of the fact that 'we are no nearer the pole than well-known German wines'. Then in 1677 appeared John Beale's *Nurseries, orchards, profitable gardens, and vineyards encouraged*. Beale readily acknowledged *The English Vineyard Vindicated* as being the definitive work on the subject: 'But yet I have much to say for the wine of the grape; though with some disparagement to our own country-man, who have done so little for it, after they have had such bright instructions, and such lively encouragements from Mr Evelyn and Mr Rose in their *English Vineyards.*'

While technically possible, and despite *The English Vineyard Vindicated* having the kudos of being endorsed by John Evelyn, for many decades vine-growing was not re-established. Yet, for the next 200 years, Rose's little book remained the definitive work. It was acknowledged as such by other writers, notably Sir Edward Barry in 1775, Francis Vispire in 1786 and William Speechly in 1790. All wrote about vines and viticulture, puzzling why British vineyards – though once viable – had become practically extinct.

What Rose's campaign had been unable to do was overcome the discrimination against English vines. As Philip Miller lamented in 1747 in *The Gardener's Dictionary*: 'Such was the Prejudice most people conceived to any Attempts of producing Wine in England that, for some Ages past, every trial of that kind has been ridiculed by the Generality of People, and at this day very few

By 1881 the dessert grape vine at Hampton Court was already 110ft long! (John Sheaf, the Twickenham Museum)

Persons will believe it possible to be effected.' A rare exception to such attitudes was the Hon. Charles Hamilton who planted a famous vineyard at Painshill, near Cobham in Surrey, in 1740. Hamilton wrote of the high quality of his produce: 'My white wine nearly resembled Champagne and as the vines grew stronger, to my great amazement, my wine had a finer flavour than the best Champagne I ever tasted.' Contemporary accounts also likened his wines to champagne, and many were surprised at its qualities, although some were less sure. The next great land-owner to indulge in vine-growing on an epic scale was the Marquis of Bute who planted a sizeable vineyard at Castel Coch near Cardiff. In 1877 the first crop was harvested, irrespective of *Punch* magazine's impression that if ever a bottle of wine were produced it would take 'one man to drink it, two to hold the victim down while the fourth pours it down his throat'! Never-theless Bute persevered. As with Hamilton the vine-growing was really only kept going by the enthusiasm of his family; and thus in 1920, several years after he died, so did the vineyard.

Inspired by Rose's book, the modern revival of English vineyards gained new impetus in 1955 when the enthusiast Major-General Sir Guy Salisbury-Jones, having planted a vineyard at Hambledon, in Hampshire, began selling the first commercially made English wine for many decades. Then in 1960 Colonel and Mrs Gore-Brown planted England's second commercial vineyard at Beaulieu. Thereafter an increasing band of vineyards were opened by owners who took advantage of the availability of more appropriate varieties and recent climate changes. Today, astonish-ingly, there are some 400 vineyards in England.

John Rose himself seems to have done rather well from his advocacy of vine-growing, claiming before his death in 1677 that 'with so plentiful a Stock of Sets and Plants of all those

Sorts which I chiefly recommend, that those who have a desire to Store their Grounds, may receive them of me at very reasonable Rates'.

Britain's oldest vine is at Hampton Court, www.hampton-court.co.uk.

Most Popular Exotic Plants and their Collectors

Collected	Finder
Cherry laurel	Pierre Belon (1518–63)
Hydrangea	Engelbert Kaempfer (1651–1715)
Wellingtonia	William Lobb (1811–94)
Forsythia	Robert Fortune (1813–80)
Crocus	Joseph Hooker (1817–1911)

Carolus Clusius's Flower Garden

An adventurous academic, Carolus Clusius was hugely influential in transforming the composition of northern European flower gardens, which before 1560 contained a limited selection of ornamental plants. As one of the first Europeans to bring plants from the wild to be grown in gardens he created a revolution of opportunity by showing how horticulture could expand beyond its preponderant concern with food and medicine. The Netherlands' position as a foremost gardening nation was established in the early seventeenth century through his pioneering horticultural work. Clusius was the most influential of all the Netherlands' scientific horticulturalists, and – unwittingly – came to be known as the principal originator of the infamous 'tulipomania' craze.

Charles de l'Ecluse – who became so keen on plant classification that he Latinised his name to Carolus Clusius – was born to a wealthy noble family at Arras, in northern France, in 1526. His early years were devoted to the study of law, but in the course of his extensive student travels his interests shifted to plant science and medicine, and by 1555 he had become a medical doctor. Clusius began exploring for plants in southern France in 1550. Then, in 1563–4, he travelled into Spain and Portugal, where he made extensive cuttings of the rare plants he discovered there (notably narcissi and Spanish irises). Much of his time was spent corresponding with, or personally meeting, many of the leading botanical scholars of the age, such as Dodonaeus, Matthias de Lobel, and John Gerard. Clusius's Spanish discoveries so made his name that he became known to other collectors, including significantly, Ogier Ghilselin de Busbecq,

Carolus Clusius (1526–1609), whose plant descriptions facilitated the growth of flower gardening in Europe. Woodcut by Jean Theodore de Bry (1528–98).

a keen gardener who was also the ambassador of the Holy Roman Emperor Ferdinand I to the Ottoman Empire of Suleiman the Magnificent, Sultan of Turkey.

In 1573 Busbecq used his influence to have Clusius appointed head of the Holy Roman Emperor's imperial medicinal gardens in Vienna. From there Clusius perfected the modus operandi of exploration and publication he had developed on his Spanish peregrination. In 1575 the house of Plantin, which specialised in botanical works, published the detailed descriptions and woodcuts from that trip; then, in 1583, they produced illustrations of the unique plantlife he discovered on an expedition to Austria–Hungary. An inveterate traveller, in 1581 he made a visit to England especially to see the plants brought back by Drake and Ralegh. But it was the tulip for which he would be remembered. In 1554 Busbecq reputedly had been the first Westerner to observe them, growing in Turkish gardens near Constantinople and the hilly town of Adrianople. He acquired some bulbs and subsequently supplied them to Clusius.

However, after fourteen years at Vienna, Clusius had to flee to Germany and then the Netherlands, a country tolerant of his Catholic faith, to seek religious sanctuary. Arriving in the Netherlands in 1593 Clusius was made a university professor of botany at Leiden, a hitherto quiet academic town several miles south of the port of Rotterdam. Leiden's 1-acre walled academic garden, the Hortus Academicus, was originally laid out in 1587 as a purely medical garden but was still one of the earliest botanical gardens in Europe (other such gardens had been established at Pisa in 1543, Padua in 1545 and Florence 1550). As in monastic gardens, medicinal herbs were grown there, leaving few opportunities for other plants because little else was known to exist. Until then the flora of European gardens was

The influential *Rariorum plantarum historia* (1601) had more than 1,000 illustrations, many of the plants never seen before such as this *Sorbus torminalis Plinii*. (Menten, *Plant and Floral Woodcuts for Designers and Craftsmen*, Dover, 1974)

essentially as it had been from time immemorial. In the seven centuries from the time of Charlemagne to that of Clusius, the total number of generally grown garden plants had increased only from forty to ninety. Furthermore, scientific classification was virtually non-existent.

All that would change at Leiden, where Clusius had effectively been made Europe's first scientific horticulturalist and taxonomist.

He revamped the university's walled garden, keeping its layout of subdivided areas but planting each with a particular variety (to assist medical students with plant identification). Small rectangular beds set out around a central pergola were edged with bricks and separated by paths of crushed white shells. Clusius now brought in plants, irrespective of their medicinal advantages, which had rarely been seen before. He drew on a lifetime of contacts and travels to import into the Netherlands many plants from the Eastern Mediterranean, Spain, Portugal, Austria and Hungary, plants such as crown imperials, hyacinths, narcissi, crocuses, Spanish and Siberian irises, windflowers, lilies and sunflowers. He opened the university's garden to the public, which caused something of a sensation.

Clusius was assisted in the Leiden garden by the head gardener, Cluyt, a skilled botanist and pharmacist from Delft who was also a famous bee-keeper and one of the first Dutchmen to publish a book on bee-keeping. From Vienna, Clusius had brought several of the Turkish tulip bulbs given him by Busbecq, and it was with Cluyt's help that he set about growing them at Leiden. Because traditionally the Turks grew tulips in hilly, well-drained areas, the growing area in the wet Leiden flatlands must have been quite inappropriate. But Cluyt evidently made some arrangement of sandy soil in the university's garden, because the tulips grew! Clusius bred and developed a private tulip collection, from which, being something of an entrepreneur, he sold specimens.

Clusius stimulated such a landslide of plants (most of them not tulips) into the Netherlands that Plantins' issue of his latest illustrated book in 1601, *Rariorum plantarum historia*, contained some 1,400 woodcuts. This was his chief work. Not only did he list in it plants by their Latin names, he also used the names by which they were commonly known in several languages. He

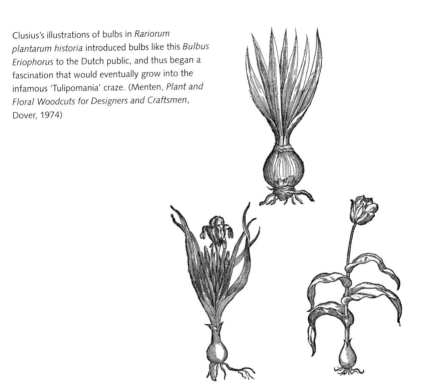

Clusius's illustrations of bulbs in *Rariorum plantarum historia* introduced bulbs like this *Bulbus Eriophorus* to the Dutch public, and thus began a fascination that would eventually grow into the infamous 'Tulipomania' craze. (Menten, *Plant and Floral Woodcuts for Designers and Craftsmen*, Dover, 1974)

described the medicinal properties of various plants, cited ancient authors such as Pliny, and gave accurate and elegant descriptions. But it was the few illustrations of tulips that he included within the work that really caught the public imagination. Prices began to rise and local gardeners broke into the academic garden and stole many of Clusius's specimen tulips. It was from those that the subsequently famous Dutch tulip-growing and bulb industry grew.

So rare were tulips in the Netherlands at this time that only the wealthy could afford them. Prices rose higher still because of an observation Clusius had made – that tulips could 'break' unpredictably (a condition later found to be caused by a virus). By the 1630s bulbs were changing hands for £400, the equivalent today of £4 million! The craze spiralled out of control until 1637 when 'tulipomania' speculators were ruined and the market for the plants suddenly collapsed.

Clusius died in 1609, still in charge of the academic garden at Leiden. His great writings and discoveries of many species were all overshadowed by the tulip craze, which brought him little profit. His consolation was that the species of shrub, Clusia, was named after him. In recent decades the Leiden garden has been reconstructed. Only some years after Clusius's death did it become apparent that tulips were not really known by that name in Turkey – their proper name there and in Iran was 'lale'. It seems that Busbecq, who had first brought them to the West, had mistaken the words of his guide, who had been comparing the shape of the flower to that of a turban (*tulipand*).

Carolus Clusius's garden, reconstructed near its original site at Leiden University, is open to the public, www.hortus.leidenuniv.nl.

John Loudon's Horticultural Journal

In 1826 appeared a new horticultural journal, the *Gardener's Magazine*. Hitherto gardening journalism had preponderantly been concerned with descriptions of plants, but with plenty of inventions and innovations in the air this new astonishingly eclectic publication created by John Claudius Loudon was a breath of fresh air. Now, for the first time, there was a magazine intended for a wider readership than the gentry alone. Loudon openly criticised gentry gardens if he thought criticism appropriate, thereby setting a precedent of independence of mind in horticultural journalism. He sought to promote various social improvements and include in the magazine's readership working gardeners, on whose behalf he humanely campaigned for better lodgings, wages and hours. He broadened minds by bringing in state-of-the-art reports from foreign correspondents, thereby making the *Gardener's Magazine* an international forum for horticultural information and ideas. The journal even had advertisements – another bright idea never seen before.

Who was this remarkable polymath? The son of a prosperous Scottish farmer, John Claudius Loudon was born in 1783 and studied arboriculture at the University of Edinburgh. Arriving in London with letters of introduction, he began his metropolitan career with the journalistic energy and flair that were to dominate the rest of his life. Prodigious books, which he illustrated himself, about public squares, plantations, hot-houses and country residences swiftly appeared, and in 1806 at only 23 years of age he was elected to the Linnean Society. However, in that year he was

John Claudius Loudon (1783–1843), the prolific horticultural writer whose ingenious mind could vault from garden tool designs to a scheme for a city environmental greenbelt. In his lifetime he wrote some 66 million words! (Loudon, *Self-instruction for Young Gardeners*, Longman, 1847)

afflicted with the first onset of the rheumatic fever that was to increasingly encroach on his physical mobility and enforce a lull in his landscaping activities. Determined to prove that the farming methods of his native Lanarkshire could profitably be applied to the south, during his convalescence at Pinner he rented a farm. Five years later he continued his innovations on a more substantial scale, acquiring Tew Lodge in Oxfordshire where he took pupils and pioneered the notion of an agricultural college. By 1812 he had made enough profit to be able to sell the farm, invest the substantial fortune and set out on a fact-finding tour through Germany, northern Europe and Moscow, which he reached when it was still smouldering from Napoleon's disastrous campaign.

Loudon returned home to find another catastrophe – his investments had failed and he was virtually ruined. Thereupon he set out to rebuild his fortune by inventing a wrought-iron glazing bar that could be used in curved sections of greenhouses, then embarking on another foreign tour, this time to Italy, France and the Low Countries collecting material for a proposed *Encyclopaedia of Gardening*. Published in 1822, the 1,500-page book covered plant culture, garden design, an international *tour d'horizon* and a history of gardening. A huge success (during Loudon's lifetime it went through six editions), it attracted considerable publicity largely thanks to his talent for using numerous woodcuts to give graphic representation to the mass of information that this garden work contained. The epic was all the more remarkable in that Loudon had compiled it in conditions of considerable physical ill health. In 1820 an operation on his fractured right arm was so bungled that it led to his addiction to the painkiller laudanum – in 1825 the arm had to be amputated nevertheless.

Loudon shrewdly recognised that a potentially lucrative market was at hand – an expanding middle class needed guidance in the

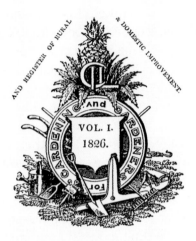

THE

GARDENER'S MAGAZINE,

AND REGISTER OF RURAL & DOMESTIC IMPROVEMENT

VOL. I.
1826.

CONDUCTED

By J. C. LOUDON, F.L.S. H.S. &c.

AUTHOR OF THE ENCYCLOPÆDIAS OF GARDENING AND OF AGRICULTURE, AND
EDITOR OF THE ENCYCLOPÆDIA OF PLANTS.

LONDON:

PRINTED FOR

LONGMAN, REES, ORME, BROWN, AND GREEN,

PATERNOSTER-ROW.

1826.

Horticultural journalism was revolutionised in 1826 by the *Gardener's Magazine*, in which Loudon targetted the expanding middle-class need for guidance in the cultivation of the gardens of their new villas. (*Gardener's Magazine* 1826 and 1840)

cultivation of their new villa gardens – and so he devised a journalised version of his reputable *Encyclopaedia* for this end. In 1826 he began publishing *Gardener's Magazine and Register of Rural and Domestic Improvement*, a pamphlet-sized journal whose purpose, Loudon declared in his inaugural editorial, was to 'disseminate new and improved information on all topics connected with horticulture, and to raise the intellect and character of those engaged in this art'. It clearly met the wants of a large class of readers, since 4,000 copies of the first number were sold within a week. By nature an encourager and facilitator, Loudon not only packed the journal with informative articles (and also advertisements) but took delight in giving illustrated descriptions of the latest gadgets and horticultural contraptions.

The *Gardener's Magazine* was the first cheap illustrated journal published for the general public, but it soon became the universal means of communication among gardeners. Hitherto there had been a few horticultural journals, but they had either specialised in esoteric botanical subjects, or had catered primarily for the gentry. Loudon strongly disapproved of such elitism. In only the second number of the work he condemned the Horticultural Society, whose affairs were then notoriously ill managed, though before the *Gardener's Magazine* no one had ventured to complain of the society publicly. Such was the breadth of his mind that in the same issue he wrote an article on the 'Self-education of Gardeners', in which he exhorted gardeners to better themselves. Soon he was a champion for improved living conditions for labourers as well as gardeners.

Another apparent factor in the magazine's success was Loudon's assemblage of a team of knowledgeable contributors, horticultural luminaries such as Donald Beaton, who went on to become perhaps the most important character in establishing the 'gardenesque' bedding system (a term Loudon himself had devised in the magazine). Overseeing this team was the phenomenally hard-working Loudon, who termed himself 'the Conductor', and in effect he wrote much of the magazine himself. In 1828 he reviewed for the magazine a futuristic novel by the writer Jane Webb, whom he fell in love with and – regardless of the twenty-four-year gap in their ages – married in 1830. Their family home was 3 Porchester Terrace, Bayswater, a villa which Loudon had designed and built in 1824. He also designed the garden himself, and readers of the *Gardener's Magazine* were kept informed of the practical aspects of the garden's subsequent evolution. Jane quickly became a prolific writer on horticultural subjects, and the Loudons were regarded as the first celebrity gardening couple and were invited to the most prestigious social occasions and houses.

Since starting the *Gardener's Magazine* Loudon had travelled to many parts of the British Isles to provide reports on the state of the country's gardens. His readers seemed to appreciate that wherever he went, diligently inspecting gardens and nurseries, he could be relied upon to speak his own mind. It was a licence to roam, which meant he would dispense praise or disapproval as he saw fit, and no garden, even one as famous as Chatsworth, would be spared his criticisms. Jane now accompanied him on these travels, and a tour he made of France and Germany in 1828 provided him with enough data for a series of articles on foreign gardens, spread over several issues. Such peregrinations made even the most timid readers think that visits to far-off gardens might somehow be possible.

For some while the *Gardener's Magazine* enjoyed a monopoly in providing aspirational lifestyle advice and practical recommendations to the British middle classes. The magazine provided the

ART OF GARDENING.

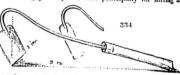

The versatile Loudon packed the *Gardener's Magazine* with useful pictures, which varied from illustrations of simple hand tools . . .

1708. *The Leicestershire or shifting-blade hoe* has the convenience of having a movable blade, and thus admitting the use of blades of different sizes. The various forms of the hoe are shown in *fig.* 332., in which *d* is the head, consisting of a socket for the blade, and a tubular socket or hose for the handle, without the blade; *b*, one of the blades not inserted in the socket; *c*, the socket with the kind of blade inserted which is used for general purposes, and more especially for hoeing between rows of drilled crops; and *a*, a socket with the blade (*b*) inserted, which is used chiefly for thinning turnips. *Fig.* 333. is a section across the socket of the full size, showing the slit (*c*) in which the blade is inserted. The use of the shifting hoe is, that a man when he goes to hoe turnips in a field may take five or six blades for his hoe in his pocket, which he can change in succession as they become dull, which they very soon do, and thus a great deal of time is spared.

1709. *The Bicton crane-necked hoes* (*fig.* 334.) are used principally for stirring the surface among growing crops where there is not room for a larger hoe. They are also used for thinning out seed beds, and they are made of various sizes, some of them being small enough for stirring the soil in pots. These hoes were invented by Mr. Barnes, gardener to Lady Rolle, at Bicton, near Exeter, and are used by him for a variety of purposes. He has them of ten or twelve different sizes, and he employs them for every kind of crop, from beds of carrots, turnips, onions, &c., in the open ground, to stirring the surface of the earth in pots and seed pans. The larger kinds are used for destroying weeds, as well as stirring the soil.

1710. *The Spanish hoe* (*fig.* 335.), lately called Lord Vernon's new tillage hoe (see *Gard. Mag.*, vol. viii. p. 689.), is a powerful implement for penetrating into hard soils; or, when made on a small scale, with a short handle (as in *fig.* 336.), it is well adapted for stirring the ground among small articles.

. . . to descriptions of how collapsible plant-boxes were constructed. (Loudon, *An Encyclopaedia of Gardening*, Longman, 1860)

ART OF GARDENING.

1837. *The annular saucer* (*fig.* 460.) is intended to defend plants placed in the centre against woodlice and slugs; the annular channel being filled with water.

1838. *The qualities and durability of pots and saucers* depend on the sort of clay and degree of burning, in which a knowledge can only be acquired by observation and experience. Pots too much burned crack and fall in pieces; and those which are not burned enough splinter or scale off with the frost and continued moisture. Porous earthenware is most congenial to the plants; but, by admitting transpiration by the sides, dries the earth within sooner. Pots made of washed clay are less porous than those of common earthenware, and, having the advantage of being more easily moulded, they

460

are consequently more beautiful in their forms, and more exact in their proportions. Glazed or stoneware pots are not congenial to plants, but they retain moisture a long time.

1839. *The galvanic plant protector* was supposed, when it was first invented, to afford a secure protection against slugs and all other similar animals; and the theory of its construction is very curious. It consists of a taper or conical ring of zinc, the top edge of which is flanged off about a quarter of an inch, and cut into numerous zigzag or vandyked points. Immediately under this pointed flange, another ring, but of copper, is neatly fitted, being exactly of the same taper as the former, and fully an inch broad, supported in its place by dots of solder in three or four places of its circumference. It was supposed that any snails and slugs that might crawl up the side of the pot would receive a galvanic shock the moment they left the zinc, and reached the copper. But, however ingenious this plan appears in theory, it was not found to answer in practice, and it is now very seldom to be met with.

1840. *The plant-box* (*figs.* 461, 462, and 463.) is a substitute for a large pot: it is of a cubical figure, and generally formed of wood, though in some cases the frame is formed

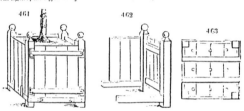

461   462   463

of cast iron, and the sides of slates cut to fit, and movable at pleasure. Such boxes are chiefly used for orange trees. The construction of those at Versailles is generally approved. Two of the opposite sides are fixed, the other two are movable, but kept in their places by a couple of iron bars with hinges, which are fastened on one side, and on the other are hooks to catch in (*fig.* 462.). By using these boxes the old earth taken out, and fresh put in at pleasure; another material advantage is, that the plants may be shifted by sliding them from one box into another without disturbing the roots.

1841. *McIntosh's orange-box* (*fig.* 461.) differs from that described above, in being tapered a little, which gives it a lighter appearance than those that are made square; it has also all its sides movable. Two of them are attached to the bottom of the box by hinges, and are kept in their places by iron bars hooked at each end, which slip into hasps fixed to the sides. The other sides (*a*) are also movable, and lift out at pleasure. These boxes afford still greater facilities than the French orange-boxes for the gardener to take them to pieces, without disturbing the trees, whenever he wishes to examine or prune their roots, to see whether they are in a proper state as regards moisture, or to remove the old, and put in fresh mould. The inside of these boxes can also be painted, or covered with pitch, as often as may be judged necessary; which will, of course, make

Loudons with a comfortable annual income of some £750, and its popularity meant its price could gradually be reduced to reach a wider audience. Indeed, from 1826, when it appeared as a quarterly, priced at 5*s*; to 1827 when it appeared as a bi-monthly and from 1831 as a monthly, the price per issue declined until in 1834 it was sold at 1*s* 2*d*. By then its success had created imitators, most significantly the *Horticultural Register*, which Joseph Paxton had been influential in founding in 1831 – partly in revenge for Loudon's waspish criticism of the gardens he superintended at Chatsworth.

Loudon coped by publishing spin-offs from the *Gardener's Magazine* – a technique he had employed in starting the magazine by adapting the format of the *Encyclopaedia of Gardening*. The first of these was *The Suburban Gardener and Villa Companion* (1838), much of the material for which had been published in the *Gardener's Magazine*. A sequel devoted to practical gardening, mostly dealing with the kitchen garden, was published in 1842 as *The Suburban Horticulturist*. Moreover, the *Gardener's Magazine* was not Loudon's only venture in journal publication. Between 1828 and 1836 he edited the *Magazine of Natural History*, and between 1834 and 1839 the *Architectural Magazine*, such was the range of his expertise.

By 1838 Loudon had made the most disastrous decision of his writing career. Rather than doing a multi-volume new *Encyclopaedia of Gardening* he chose to conduct a survey of all the trees grown in the British Isles. It was a monumental project, on a scale never before attempted. At his own expense he employed some 800 correspondents and a squad of 7 artists, all of whom needed to travel far and demanded to be paid for their illustrations in advance. The eight-volume definitive *Arboretum et fruticetum Britannicum* was released in 1838 but failed dismally, which meant Loudon was some £10,000 in debt and hounded by his creditors.

Desperate to escape bankruptcy, Loudon was forced to resume his former trade as a landscape architect. It so happened that during the 1830s he had published a series of articles in the *Gardener's Magazine* describing existing cemeteries and proposing new design solutions. So now, in time of need, he was well placed to take on work designing cemeteries for Cambridge, Southampton and Bath, and he even published a book on the subject. In fact some of the other design works he undertook in the latter part of his life were among his finest achievements, most specifically the public parks he designed for Gravesend in 1835, and Derby Arboretum (1839). In 1832 he had produced designs, published in the *Gardener's Magazine*, for gigantic hothouses at the Birmingham Botanic Gardens. Those plans were never accepted by the local authority there, so it must have been infuriating for him when in 1836 Joseph Paxton, to much public acclaim, built something less grand at Chatsworth. Ever the popularist, one of the causes Loudon had always advocated was the establishment of public parks for Britain's rapidly expanding cities. Indeed, as long ago as 1829 he had published in the *Gardener's Magazine* a plan for the controlled expansion of London by means of a 'green belt' system around the capital, consisting of 1-mile-wide concentric belts of urban development separated by half-mile-wide belts of countryside that could act as breathing zones.

To stave off financial ruin, Loudon continued to write at a frantic pace. His last book, *Self-instruction for Young Gardeners*, he was dictating to his wife until just hours before his death in December 1843. The *Gardener's Magazine* immediately ceased publication, but it had changed the face of British horticultural journalism. Abroad, too, it was influential. From the outset, many

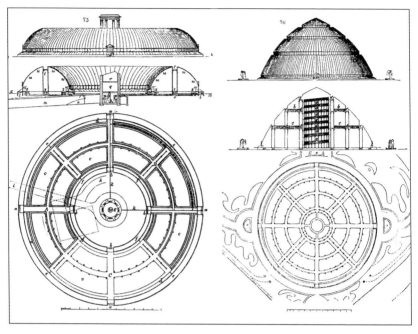

An ingenious horticultural architect, Loudon published in the magazine his plans for gigantic 200ft diameter greenhouses for the Birmingham Botanic Gardens, in 1832. (*Gardener's Magazine*, 1832)

of its articles had been translated into French and German, while in the United States, America's leading landscape architect, Andrew Jackson Downing, applied many of Loudon's ideas in his designs, books and the magazine he founded there in 1845, *The Horticulturalist*. Loudon, who during his lifetime wrote an estimated 60 to 66 million words, had been not only the most prolific gardening writer ever, but by his know-how of the technical and aesthetic aspects of gardening, architecture and agriculture, he was the last polymath to have a grasp of all those subjects.

Outside the Loudons' house, 3 Porchester Terrace, London W2, there is a blue plaque. The Derby Arboretum remains the most significant public garden improved by Loudon, www.derbyarboretum.co.uk.

Martin Hope Sutton's Packet Seeds

The quality of British horticulture was enhanced in the mid-nineteenth century by the Berkshire tycoon Martin Hope Sutton. Hitherto, gardeners had been required to make do with merchants selling corruptly adulterated seeds. By establishing his firm as virtually the first to test all seeds for germination, Sutton set high standards that eventually transformed the seed industry. Sutton's other achievement was to pioneer selling packet seeds to gardeners via mail order, which reinforced his distinctiveness in being the first seedsman to sell reliable top-quality seeds.

The story of the Sutton dynasty really commences with Martin's father, John Sutton (1777–1863), who established a corn milling and merchant's business called the House of Sutton in Reading's King Street in 1806. It appeared to do well in the latter years of the Napoleonic wars when corn prices were high. Then in 1814 the corn harvest failed and the prospect of a return to peace ended the long wartime agricultural boom. Within months the financial collapse of John Sutton's bankers in Reading, and then a trading house in London to which he had been consigning extensive quantities of flour, pushed the business to the verge of calamity. On the birth of a son on 15 March 1815, John Sutton, being more of an optimist than a realist at that time of financial despair, had him christened 'Martin Hope', with the ambition that the fledgling would eventually embark upon a profession more secure than agriculture.

Irrespective of his father's wishes – or perhaps in deliberate defiance of them – as a child Martin Hope Sutton developed a precociously intense interest in plants and was soon eagerly studying practical books on flowers and forage plants. At the risk of parental disapproval, books on plants would be smuggled into the house, and in the early morning, before the household rose, the garden would be furtively used as an experimental ground for comparative trials of seeds.

The family business had somehow continued but by 1827 was so deteriorating that Martin, despite being only 12 years old, had to abandon his vocation to be a missionary and begin work. By then John Sutton had increasingly sought to immunise himself against the firm's financial plight by excessive drinking every afternoon. In such absences his millers would slacken off work, and Martin, who was supposed to oversee them, quickly became frustrated by the wastefulness of his father's inattention to the details of the business. The firm marketed turnip and other agricultural seeds, but unprofitably. Their main trade was in corn, flour, malt and hops, but Martin soon decided that this part of the business could not be developed either. Could far better returns, he wondered, be achieved from selling garden seeds?

Adhering to the conventional view that horticultural seeds were somehow beneath the dignity or scope of a milling and corn seed establishment, John Sutton refused to listen. Nevertheless, in 1828 he begrudgingly allowed Martin use of a small patch of the family garden at Forbury, with the proviso that all study of horticultural books, sowing and harvesting seeds in the garden, and putting them into packets must be done only outside working hours. Undaunted in his determination to begin selling garden seeds, the

Martin Hope Sutton (1815–1901), the Berkshire entrepreneur who revolutionised the garden seed trade. (*The Christian*, 10 October 1901)

13-year-old Martin used his own money to buy in seeds. Having sowed these he later collected the harvests, which he added to his stock of treasures and consigned them to a wooden chest he had made himself. The size of a suitcase, measuring just 17in high, 14in wide and 7in deep, the chest had forty-two compartments and became the foundation of what would eventually be a thriving business empire.

Significantly, Martin added to his know-how by making fact-finding and trading visits to all the nursery establishments in the neighbourhood. Several decades later he recalled to the *Reading Standard* that a not untypical such tour might be 'To Brown's Tulips at Slough, Ronald's at Brentford, the Knaphill and Woking Nurseries, and Waterers at Bagshot. I walked back during the night in order to be at my desk at the proper time in the morning.' That expedition was a round trip of well over 70 miles, made on foot. Indeed, to Martin Sutton it was nothing remarkable that he should walk 25 miles home during the night to start work at 7 a.m. The business progress that he made meant that in 1831 an account was opened for him with a London wholesale seed firm.

For centuries the London seed merchants had been a dominant and corrupting force in the seed trade. It was they who maintained the crooked tradition of reducing the germinating quality of seeds by introducing withered ones in a certain fixed proportion – sometimes even cleverly killed by a special machine. For example, it was quite proper to mix killed rapeseed, worth less than 3*d* per pound, with cabbage, broccoli and other round seeds worth many shillings per pound. So prevalent was that practice of bulking out that it was not considered reprehensible. Seedsmen justified it by the plea that customers always sowed too thickly, so if an average of three-quarters were growing seeds, no failure of crop or loss would be sustained! Buyers, of course, were aware of this fact, and if they particularly wanted the unadulterated article they had to stipulate 'net' seed, and to pay a higher price for it than the printed list quotation. Uniquely, Martin resolved to have no hand in this practice of reducing seeds by the mixture of dead seed.

The immediate effect of Martin Sutton's business practice of sowing only new seeds, free from any admixture of old or killed seeds, was startling. The crops grown by Sutton's customers attracted the attention of their neighbours, and so by word of mouth Sutton's business increased by leaps and bounds. In 1832 Martin and his three sisters made 8,700 brown paper bags and wrote out all the seed labels by hand. It had initially been a struggle to build up the business in garden seeds, but by 1839 those products accounted for some 42 per cent of the stocks of predominantly agricultural seeds. In 1836 Martin, aged 21, became a partner with his father at the House of Sutton, and promptly phased out the corn side of the business. The firm became Sutton & Sons, and that year moved from Reading's King Street to grander premises, a double-fronted tenanted shop with large windows prominently situated overlooking the town's vegetable and general market. Shrewdly conscious of the need to

Keen to capitalise on his trustworthy image, Martin Hope Sutton took over this prominent shop in Reading's Market Place in 1836 and called it the 'Seed Establishment'. In 1858, when he received a Royal Warrant, he renamed it the 'Royal Seed Establishment'. (Suttons' Consumer Products Ltd)

develop the firm's trustworthy image, Martin audaciously painted across the frontage the words 'Seed Establishment'.

To secure more customers, in 1832 Martin Sutton produced one of the earliest ever seed catalogues, which at first he had distributed locally by hand in the form of a printed leaflet. But what really did so much to expand the family business was the creation of the penny post. A radical plan for a national penny post to overcome the inefficiencies of various regions setting differing postal rates was first mooted in a pamphlet in 1837 by a Kidderminster inventor, Rowland Hill. Soon endorsed by a committee of the House of Commons, Hill's scheme – and the new adhesive penny black stamp – became fully operational in January 1840, enabling any letter weighing less than half an ounce to be dispatched anywhere in Britain for just one penny. Simultaneously there began a huge increase in public enthusiasm for transferring money via postal orders (189,000 were issued in 1839, and 7.5 million in 1861). Suttons, having created a mail-order system, thanks to the penny post, each year sent out thousands of Martin's free catalogues (which now contained order forms), and could immediately execute the resulting orders by return of post – and thereby, with their efficiency, increase customer goodwill. Not only was this the perfect time for the expansion of Suttons, their premises, in Reading, were also fortuitously placed. Aware of this, in March 1841 Martin was at Reading station to witness the departure of the first train to London. Ever the salesman, he even took advantage of the occasion to sell flower seed to passers-by and spectators! The railway would subsequently become crucial to the Sutton business, bringing in large consignments of seeds and bulbs and sending off bulky orders too heavy to go by post.

Convinced he was on to a winner with his emphasis on selling only quality seeds, in 1838 Martin Sutton arranged for the company to acquire its own nursery grounds in Reading. That year he began selling greenhouse plants, many of the bulbs coming from approved local nurseries, and some from Holland. Then in 1840 a decision was taken to establish a laboratory, where Martin developed a system of germinating seeds in a heated environment and afterwards testing them under natural con-ditions in the open air. In future decades all the principal seed businesses would have their own seed-testing laboratories, but to Sutton belonged the honour of being one of the first firms to themselves test all seed for germination and purity under glass and in the open ground before any was sold. When the Seeds Act became law in 1869 Suttons' laboratory was one of the earliest to receive an official government licence.

Ironically, the disastrous failure of Ireland's potato crop and the resultant 1847 Irish famine hugely assisted the expansion of Sutton's business. For the first time it enabled Martin to prove on a large scale that the experiments he had made in cultivating, adapting and selecting plants for ornamentation and food were capable of being tuned to practical account in the public good. That year he contacted the government and urged that the devastated potato fields be at once sown with his turnip, beetroot and cabbage seeds (which by quick growth ought soon to mitigate the severity of the famine). The wisdom of planting those substitutes was immediately accepted by the authorities and extensive orders for vegetable seeds were placed with the firm. A very substantial increase in business resulted, and Suttons became renowned not merely in the southern counties of England, but throughout the United Kingdom.

At about this time Martin's innovative work was brought to the attention of the royal family via General Viscount Bridport and the Marquis of Hertford, who were equerries at Windsor. Upon their recommendation Martin obtained a personal introduction to Prince Albert, and thence the additional privilege of supplying seeds for the home farms at Windsor and elsewhere, and also specialist grasses for the grounds at Osborne House, the new royal residence completed on the Isle of Wight in 1851. At Windsor, Martin came to be often summoned by Queen Victoria to advise on the gardens, and exhibitions of the Prince Consort's Association there, mounted for the benefit of cottagers and estate workers, again brought him into contact with the Queen. On one

Reforms of the postal system enabled Sutton & Sons to develop a huge mail-order seed business that advertised its products in horticultural magazines such as *Gardening Illustrated*. (Museum of Garden History)

occasion she presented him with a pair of large goats, and every year until her death she sent him a present at Christmas. The royal family's commercial patronage was formally confirmed in 1858 when the first warrants of appointments as seedsmen to the Queen and Prince of Wales were granted to Suttons; Martin's response was to opportunistically subtitle the business the 'Royal Seed Establishment', which appeared wherever they promoted their products, be it on metal signs in railway stations or full-page advertisements in gardening magazines.

Meanwhile, the service offered by Suttons for domestic gardeners continued to improve. Their mail-order catalogue, which had been issued free since 1840, was greatly enlarged in 1856 and issued as *Sutton's Amateur's Guide in Horticulture*, then subsequently published annually. With its descriptions of flowers and vegetables and the proper methods of cultivating them, it became something of an institution and as great a favourite with skilled gardeners as with amateurs – especially because of its vivid illustrations. Suttons were quite possibly the earliest horticultural concern to use photographs: also established in Reading was, from 1843, one of the founding inventors of photographic processing, William Fox-Talbot. A paper Martin Sutton produced for the Royal Agricultural College and subsequently (from 1863) republished many times as *Laying Down Land to Permanent and Temporary Pasture*, advising on what grass seeds grew best on particular soils, influentially established Suttons as a leading supplier of such specialist seeds for tennis courts, bowling greens and sports fields. The paper led to a huge development in Sutton exports to the empire (indeed half of New Zealand's sheep pastureland was reputedly grown from Sutton seeds). To reliably cope with export demands Martin ingeniously arranged for seeds to be shipped overseas preserved in 400-gallon tanks. In 1872, when the firm moved to huge new 6-acre premises in Reading, they were acknowledged to be Britain's largest suppliers of seeds.

In recognition of his success Martin was believed to have been offered a knighthood and even a chance to stand for Parliament, which he politely declined. A humble man who never forgot he had built a fortune at the price of abandoning his vocation for missionary work, he established several charitable institutions for Reading's needy. By way of example he cured his father's alcoholism. Though kindly, his strength of character was such that in business matters he was mistrustful of his four children, whom he had made partners in the company, and on one occasion berated them for building over-extravagant marquees for horticultural shows. Communiqués would even be rattled off to them concerning matters of propriety, such as a Sutton girl who

In 1872 Martin Hope Sutton moved his premises to a 6-acre site at Reading, and was soon claiming to have created the world's largest seed business. (Corley, *Berkshire Archaeological Journal*, 1998–2003)

had shown too much leg while bicycling in the town! For many decades after his death in 1901 Sutton & Sons remained a successful family firm. In 1965, very much in Martin Sutton's innovative tradition, they became the first company to offer foil seed packets to amateur gardeners.

Various ingenious seed sorting and sowing devices can be seen at the Museum of Garden History, www.museumgardenhistory.org, and Museum of English Rural Life, www.ruralhistory.org.

Harry Veitch's Chelsea Flower Show

Now widely perceived to be the world's greatest flower show, the Chelsea Flower Show in fact came about in 1913 practically by accident – and, crucially, one which the Royal Horticultural Society were persuaded to capitalise on by the respected plantsman Sir Harry Veitch.

At variance with its established image, subsequent to its founding by a group of gentlemen in Hatchard's bookshop in 1804 for the purpose of 'horticulture pure and simple', the Royal Horticultural Society (RHS) suffered decades of turbulence and shifting fortunes. In 1818 it began an experimental garden in Kensington; then, four years later, it leased 33 acres from the Duke of Devonshire at Chiswick. However, because in that era it was considered unbecoming to hound members to make regular subscriptions, the society drifted toward bankruptcy. In one particularly severe crisis in 1859 its irreplaceable collections of books and drawings were sold. Then, in 1861, the society acquired another garden, at Kensington Gore, which it then wastefully furbished with statues, tennis courts and other non-horticultural features. From the society's earliest years it had been usual for Fellows to bring specimens of plants to meetings, and later competitions were held. These were so popular that in 1883 John Lindley, the famous botanist and sometime editor of the *Gardener's Chronicle*, suggested holding a larger show under canvas at Chiswick. Those Chiswick shows, complete with refreshments and military bands, were popular and struck a pleasantly democratic note, which is gardening's great social virtue. The *Gardener's Magazine* approvingly reported, 'the principal part of the English aristocracy are present and mix indiscriminately with the tradesman, the mechanic and the gardener'.

However, in 1888 the society consisted of only 1,108 Fellows and was again in a perilous financial state. That year the RHS arranged with the benchers of the Inner Temple to hold a show in their grounds between Fleet Street and the River Thames. According to Hester Marsden-Smedley, in her book *The Chelsea Flower Show*, although it was the society's largest and most ambitious show to date, its success indicated the turn of the tide in the RHS's fortunes. The tradition of a May show was established and, in spite of many difficulties such as bad weather, exhibitors and visitors grew in number annually until 1911. Several of the barristers (benchers) considered it fun to be able to nip out from chambers at lunchtime and mingle with the stallholders. However, with many members and tenants of the Inner Temple becoming more and more uneasy with the rising levels of disruption and noise, increasingly finicky restrictions were imposed, such as the banning of advertisements fixed to the garden railings without consent and the banning of all beverages in the refreshment tent other than tea. As one grumpy Inner

Temple lawyer reputedly commented, 'moist plants and dry law were not really natural allies'.

Although May 1913 was the date of the first Chelsea Flower Show as such, its forerunner was of major importance. This was the Royal International Horticultural Exhibition of 22–30 May 1912, a lavish one-off event for the sake of which the RHS agreed to cancel its own show at the Temple that year. The directors of that international show decided it should be held in the grounds of the Royal Hospital at Chelsea. In fact there had been a flower show in the Royal Hospital grounds once before – the RHS's own summer show, in June 1905. However, this was comparatively small, making little impact compared with the regular RHS shows at the Temple. It was widely felt by exhibitors and officials alike that Chelsea was too far from the centre of London: would people take the trouble to journey there on the underground, as they had done to the more accessible Charing Cross for Temple shows?

The key figure in quelling such doubts about distance and insisting that the Royal Hospital grounds were ideal was the RHS's vice-president Harry Veitch – the great-grandson of the distinguished nurseryman John Veitch, who in 1800 had established a nursery at Killerton, near Exeter. The Veitch dynasty became internationally renowned for their far-sighted sponsorship of famous plant hunters. The growing reputation of the firm brought Harry to London, where in 1853 they had acquired the commercial nursery of Knight and Perry in Chelsea, which became known as the Royal Exotic Nursery. An intricate maze of glasshouses and flowerbeds that stretched over several acres, it specialised in exotic plants. Harry, who had trained at the Vilmorin–Andrieux nurseries in France, was himself a skilled hybridiser of orchids and as such had helped organise the 1866

Sir Harry Veitch, whose recommendation established the Chelsea Flower Show's traditional Thames-side venue. (Royal Horticultural Society)

International Horticultural Exhibition and Botanical Congress, at South Kensington. Although he had retired from the firm in 1900, and was already in his seventy-second year, his experience of the 1866 event was much relied upon in the preparations for the 1912 exhibition.

The 1912 Royal International Exhibition was, however, experimental and on a very bold scale. While the idea had come from within the RHS, the society had decided to remain discreetly in the background. So a small public company was formed, with twenty-six directors under the presidency of the Duke of Portland.

The great horticultural firms were represented, and gave money and services generously; and, from the first, working gardeners were involved. The organisation was conducted with such secrecy that even newspaper gardening correspondents had scarcely an idea what was afoot until only a week before George V opened the Royal International Horticultural Exhibition on 22 May 1912. Visitors were stunned by the setting in the grounds of the Royal Hospital. Sir Christopher Wren's dignified hospital building provided a fitting backcloth while the grounds were an ideal location for displays of gardens and plants. Carriages could 'set down' at the dignified south entrance, while pedestrians, most of whom travelled by public transport, were admitted through the north entrance. Unlike the Temple setting, there was a charming sense of being in a tranquil garden set apart from the bustle of the capital. Another memorable feature was the tents – believed to be the largest ever erected – and lit by electricity!

Attendance exceeded all expectation. Many were impressed that there was so much more to see than at the Inner Temple: in the Royal Hospital grounds there were some 240 exhibitors (twice as many as at the Inner Temple) and the 23 acres there were three times as large. For the 1913 event the RHS flirted with the idea of moving their spring show to Holland Park, where Lady Ilchester had provisionally agreed a fee of £250 for the use of the grounds of her mansion. Yet although the benchers insisted on even more restrictions it still seemed assured that the RHS would resume their show at the Inner Temple in 1913. However, Harry Veitch insisted that the phenomenal success of the international exhibition had proved that people were prepared to travel to Chelsea and was determined that Chelsea should become the venue for the 1913 spring show. He finally persuaded the society's leading personages to that point of view, and in July

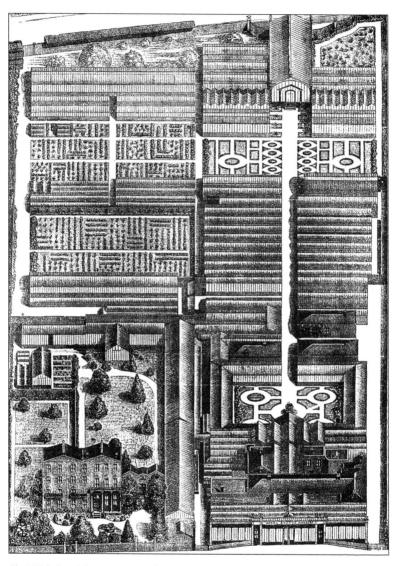

The Veitch dynasty's own commercial nursery nearby at Chelsea. (Veitch, *Hortus Veitchii*, Veitch, 1906)

1912 the RHS met with the Royal Hospital to discuss terms for a fourteen-year agreement. In August 1912 the RHS Council approved the agreement and committed the RHS to a horrifically tight schedule – to prepare the site from scratch each year in just two weeks!

The centrepiece of the first great flower show at Chelsea 1913 was a gigantic marquee, 300ft long and 275ft wide. Having it ready in time seemed a daunting task, but Piggotts of Ongar, the society's tent contractors, had long experience of providing the Royal Navy with canvas sails, and that skill proved invaluable in having the huge tent hoisted into position when required. It was acclaimed a star attraction. Visitors were overwhelmed by the great tent's brilliant masses of azaleas and rhododendrons, its profusion of roses and carnations, and the wealth of the great bank of other flowers which, facing east and west, ran almost the entire length of the tent. Indeed, outweighing by far the organisational success of the first Chelsea Show was its horticultural excellence. New plants were increasingly being introduced to Britain and exhibitors competed with each other to display those to best advantage. Orchids – of which Veitch was an expert – were displayed more lavishly than almost any other plant. At the end of May 1913 the *Gardeners' Chronicle* concluded that the Chelsea Show that year had been the most profitable in the RHS's history, with an income of £3,000 (the Temple show had produced a meagre £1,400 in 1911). The journal enthused: 'The Chelsea site should become as nearly perfect as is possible to mortal affairs to be.'

Nevertheless, in subsequent years the RHS fleetingly dabbled with ideas of moving their spring show to other sites, such as Wembley, Lambeth Palace and, further still, Lady Ilchester's grounds at Holland Park. Yet the Royal Hospital venue somehow had a special magic. Each year visitors were drawn there by a love of plants and gardens; but what also really counted at Chelsea was royal patronage, which helped ensure that the show was an event in the social calendar that could not be ignored. Year by year the event somehow evolved into a national institution with its own idiosyncratic customs, such as the selling off of artefacts and plants on the final day; and with it the delight of visitors in conspicuously taking home their bargains on the underground. The term 'cash and carry' is said to have originated at the Chelsea Flower Show. The show could also be relied upon to be a showcase for the very latest horticultural inventions, such as the sensational Webb radio-controlled lawnmower exhibited there in 1959. Media coverage of Chelsea – it was first televised in 1958 – resulted in many more visitors wanting to come and see for themselves the most important annual horticultural event in Britain.

As for the innovative Harry Veitch, his accomplished arranging of the forerunning 1912 exhibition was rewarded that year with a knighthood. Ironically, the creation of the Chelsea Flower Show (and thereby a foundation for a sustained recovery in the fortunes of the RHS), coincided with a sharp and terminal decline in the fortunes of the Veitch dynasty. In 1914 their famous nursery in Chelsea was closed and soon built over. Sir Harry died without any successors in 1924, bequeathing a massive art collection to the Royal Albert Memorial Museum in Exeter. The last of the Veitch nurseries ceased trading in 1969; although, in tribute to Harry Veitch's achievement in establishing for the RHS the world's most famous flower show, in 1988, on the seventy-fifth anniversary of the first Chelsea Show several of the participating organisations and companies recreated their original 1913 exhibits.

Elsie Wagg's National Gardens Scheme

The 'Yellow Book' guide to the National Gardens Scheme is now such an established feature of horticultural life it is surprising to know that in 1926, when the idea of enabling the general public to visit private gardens was first mooted, the proposition seemed daringly revolutionary. That June, during a meeting of the National Memorial to Queen Alexandra women's committee, Elsie Wagg, a representative of the Queen's Nursing Institute, radically proposed: 'We've got all these beautiful gardens in this country and hardly anyone sees them except the owners and their friends – why don't we ask some of them to open next year for the Appeal?'

In fact it was more of a concern for people's well-being than the care of plants that led to the creation of the National Gardens Scheme. Some of that originates from Liverpool in 1859 when one William Rathbone, a wealthy businessman, hired a trained nurse to care for his dying wife at home. This was such a comfort to his family that it made him consider the plight of the city's sick poor, for whom there was no such provision. Having retained the services of this nurse that she might tend the poor in their own homes, Rathbone also got nurses to work in other deprived areas of Liverpool, which he divided into 'districts', each with an honorary 'lady superintendent'. From this small beginning stemmed the district nursing service. It spread first to Manchester and then to London, and to other huge cities with problems similar to those of Liverpool. At an early stage Rathbone enlisted the help of Florence Nightingale and later of Queen Victoria, who took a keen interest in nursing. Thus the district nursing service was born, which grew to become in 1887 Queen Victoria's Jubilee Institute for Nurses (subsequently renamed the Queen's Institute of District Nursing (QNI)), which conducted training and set standards. Victoria's patronage was succeeded by that of her daughter-in-law Queen Alexandra and subsequent to her death in 1925, on 7 January the QNI launched the Queen Alexandra's Memorial Fund to further the development of the district nursing service and provide for retired nurses.

Quite how Elsie Wagg formulated the ingenious idea of proposing a mass opening of gardens is a mystery. Indeed, not much is known of her own personal circumstances other than that she was a Sussex high society belle. In 1893 a stunningly elegant oil painting of Elsie was completed by the American portraitist John Singer Sargent. Her home was The Hermitage, the merchant-banking Wagg family's country mansion on the edge of East Grinstead. She may have been inspired by her experience of tending to the wounded during the First World War, or her reading in October 1926 in the letters pages of *Country Life* of the Earl of Carnarvon's appeal to garden owners to urgently send packets of seeds to families of Albanian refugees.

Elsie Wagg's proposal was more of an innovation than an invention. Before her scheme, garden visits had been a passion only for a well-connected few who obtained access by written request, guaranteed by letters of introduction. Precedents of the public being allowed access to private gardens were few. The impoverished Earl of Harrington in the 1850s charged visitors to see his gardens at Elvaston Castle. Stowe became the first garden to have a guidebook. Perhaps Elsie Wagg knew of another Sussex grande dame, Lady Margaret Loder, of Leonardslee near Horsham, who in 1924 had reputedly opened, for a very short time, her extensive ornamental tree and shrub garden to the public to raise money (she raised £170). Elsewhere, open days were virtually unheard of outside of their immediate locality,

Elsie Wagg, the Sussex socialite who in 1926 devised the brilliant system of raising funds for needy district nurses by opening private gardens to the public. (The National Gardens Scheme)

unless they were listed in esoteric horticultural publications such as the *Gardeners' Chronicle* – and even then they would be known of only by well-to-do gardeners. So Wagg's idea of extending that garden visiting pastime to the general public and donating the proceeds to charity was indeed a brainwave. It was poised to combine the nation's obsession with gardening with the natural curiosity for what was happening on the other side of the fence. According to *Country Life* of 18 June 1927, 'The privacy of a garden is half its magic. Make it public, nationalise it, and not only is the mystery gone, but the motive impulse that keeps it a living work of art.'

The General Strike must have made the timing of the initiative seem inappropriate. Surely if there were perceived to be a hint of social revolution in the air it could not be realistically envisaged that the owners of the great houses would agree to throw open their garden doors to the simmering multitudes? The reaction of the committee is unrecorded, but Elsie was fortunate to find a supporter in Lady Hilda March (later Duchess of Richmond and Gordon), the chatelaine of Goodwood. A matriarch with formidable powers of persuasion, she formed a committee of lady superintendents and set to work with her contact book. Rightly, she instinctively calculated that the friendly rivalry between the owners of the great houses was a factor that would fuel the idea. But how could she best get things moving? The answer was to go directly to the top. Crucially, King George V consented to participate in the scheme by throwing open to the public the gardens at Sandringham. Henceforth, those who might have wavered willing agreed to do likewise.

It was agreed that the participating gardens would open their gates during the Whitsuntide holiday in early June 1927, and charge one shilling a head to raise money for the Memorial Fund. The list of 349 gardens that opened that month reads like an extract from *Debrett's Peerage*. It included horticultural treasures such as Blenheim Palace, Brocket Hall, Burghley House, Hatfield House, Highclere and Madresfield. Special arrangements were made with rail and bus companies for the excursions and an estimated 164,000 people, including many visitors from the Dominions and the United States, took advantage of the unprecedented opportunity to view so many of the country's finest private gardens. Elsie Wagg's idea was so well supported that many other gardens joined in, and on 24 June *The Times* reported that the 'Garden Scheme' programme was being continued throughout July and August. Unexpectedly, many who took advantage of the scheme derived as much pleasure from seeing the exterior features of the houses as they did from the adored gardens. According to Erica Hunningher, in her book *A Nuturing Nature*, altogether an astonishing 609 gardens opened that year, raising £8,191.

So enthusiastic was the response that summer that Elsie Wagg's committee realised these garden openings could be a permanent means of helping to fund district nursing. The whole machinery of what quickly became known as the 'National Gardens Scheme' (NGS) was handed over to the Queen's Institute of District Nursing. More gardens opened in 1928, and every year thereafter; and in 1932 as many as 1,079 private gardens in England and Wales opened to the public to support the scheme. Lesser members of the royal family facilitated the early growth of support. Princess Mary followed her brother the King's example and opened Harewood House in Yorkshire in 1928; the Duke of Kent opened his garden at Coppins, at Iver, in Buckinghamshire; and Princess Alice opened at Barnwell Manor, Northamptonshire.

Most Popular Gardens

Place	Visitors (2003)
Hampton Court Palace	1,300,000
Kew	1,079,000
Alnwick	500,000
Wakehurst Place	389,000
Stourhead	357,000

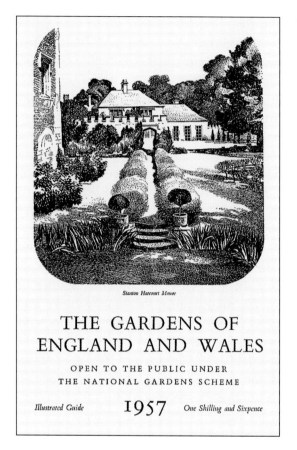

Stanton Harcourt Manor

THE GARDENS OF
ENGLAND AND WALES

OPEN TO THE PUBLIC UNDER
THE NATIONAL GARDENS SCHEME

Illustrated Guide   1957   *One Shilling and Sixpence*

The distinctive Yellow Book annual guide to the National Gardens Scheme was conspicuous for its cover – a tradition the distinguished illustrator Rowland Hilder established in 1954. (The National Gardens Scheme)

Other crowd-pulling gardens were those of famous horticultural personalities such as William Robinson, the author of *The English Flower Garden*; and Ellen Willmott and Vita Sackville-West. On 23 August 1939 the public were even allowed by Winston Churchill to visit the grounds at Chartwell.

Although the National Gardens Scheme's emblematic Yellow Book has long been an annual bestseller, its distinctive format took a while to evolve. Initially, the only written guide to all the NGC's gardens was a booklet with a 5,000 print run. In 1931 the first guide in book form appeared when the Kynoch press did an illustrated list of participating gardens, with an introduction by the architectural editor of *Country Life*, Christopher Hussey (a tradition he continued until 1939). It had a green cover and cost one shilling. Despite 3 million unemployed and the country being in a state of economic collapse, 10,000 copies of the 1934 guide were sold and £12,255 was raised. That annual publication, *The Gardens of England and Wales Open for Charity*, appeared with a yellow cover for the first time in 1949, and subsequently became commonly known as the Yellow Book. It also became traditional for the covers to be decorated with enchanting woodcuts by eminent artists – from 1954 to 1964, for example, by the book illustrator Rowland Hilder. In line with the voluntary nature of the scheme's operation, for many years the Yellow Book was produced unpaid by Rachel Crawshay, on a manual typewriter in a small flat in London's Lower Belgrave Street.

In 1948 when the National Health Service and local authorities took over responsibility for district nursing it seemed that the Gardens Scheme might no longer be necessary. But other worthy causes were found. At Vita Sackville-West's suggestion, in 1949 the NGS undertook to contribute to a Joint Gardens Committee of the National Trust and Royal Horticultural Society. The Garden Fund's purpose was the preservation of certain gardens of historic and national importance, and, with some financial assistance from the NGS, that year the National Trust acquired Hidcote. For the Gardens Scheme the alliance with the Joint Gardens Committee became valuable because, in return for the donations, from thereon the National Trust provided it with much-needed continuity in the form of reliable openings and promotional opportunities. Of much help also to the NGS was the publicity provided by the BBC and motoring organisations such as the Automobile Association.

Unbeknown to the viewing public, a recurring concern of the NGS was the reluctance of all too many owners of the grand houses to commit to routinely opening their gardens each year. For them the best encouragement was provided by the lady superintendents. Retitled Honorary County Organisers in 1931, they were the most critical components in the organisational structure as transferred from William Rathbone's district nursing command structure and Elsie Wagg's original 1927 Memorial Committee. For decades those dames of the shires safeguarded the scheme's social kudos, usually permitting only interesting old-moneyed gardens of quality in the sacred Yellow Book. Their power of veto could instantly bar the progress of the socially ambitious among the keepers of the gardens they inspected. Nevertheless, it was also by means of their formidable powers of persuasion that the better crowd-pulling private gardens were kept from dropping out of the scheme. The leader of those unsung heroines for twenty-eight years was Lady Daphne Herald, the Gardens Scheme's longest-serving chairperson (1951–79), who reputedly once said, 'A garden must always have some treasures to be shared with visitors.'

So simple was the universal appeal of Elsie Wagg's original concept, the idea spread far and wide. Garden schemes were established in Scotland, in 1931; Australia, in 1987; the United States, in 1989; Belgium, in 1989; then Japan, in 2001. In recent years the NGS has been taking on increasing numbers of small, indeed fairly ordinary, gardens – a bold move almost as radical as Elsie Wagg's first proposal, which has meant that the NGS has extended its coverage to some 3,500 gardens, while increasing its number of visitors. Contrary to the presumption of the scheme's 1927 founders, the public are just as enthusiastic to explore the gardens of households in the suburbs.

In 1984 the increasing popularity of the scheme made it possible to further extend its charitable work by assisting Macmillan Cancer Relief with funds for training Macmillan Nurses in the continuing care of cancer patients. Although it has donated to other nursing and horticultural funds, the Macmillan has become the main financial beneficiary of its activities, and in 2005 the scheme successfully collected £1.8 million. Aged 73, Elsie Wagg died in 1949. She had been awarded an MBE for her work in creating the National Gardens Scheme; but her real reward is that the scheme still continues to prosper.

Further Reading

The research for this book was chiefly done at the Royal Botanic Gardens, Kew; Royal Horticultural Society; British Library; and Wellcome Institute for the History of Medicine.

General

Adams, William H., *The French Garden, 1500–1800*, Scolar Press, 1979

Beeton, Isabella, *The Book of Gardening Management*, Ward Lock, 1872

Bridgeman, Thomas, *The American Gardener's Assistant*, Wood, 1867

Brown, Jane, *Eminent Gardeners*, Viking, 1990

——, *The English Garden Through the Twentieth Century*, Garden Art, 1999

Carter, Tom, *The Victorian Garden*, Bell and Hyman, 1984

Clifford, Derek, *A History of Garden Design*, Faber & Faber, 1962

Coats, Alice, *Flowers and Their Histories*, Hulton, 1956

Courtier, Jane, *Gardening as it Was*, Batsford, 1995

Elliott, Brent, *Victorian Gardens*, Batsford, 1986

Fisher, John, *The Origins of Garden Plants*, Constable, 1982

Fletcher, H.R., *The Story of the Royal Horticultural Society*, Oxford, 1969

Girling, Richard, *The Making of the English Garden*, Macmillan, 1988

Hadfield, B., Harling, R., and Highton, L., *British Gardeners: A Biographical Dictionary*, Zwemmer, 1980

Hadfield, Miles, *Pioneers in Gardening*, Routledge, 1955

——, *A History of British Gardening*, John Murray, 1960

Hellyer, A., *Shell Guide to Gardens*, Heinemann, 1977

Hobhouse, Penelope, *Plants in Garden History*, Pavilion Books, 1992

——, *The Story of Gardening*, Dorling Kindersley, 2002

Holmes, Caroline, *Icons of Garden Design*, Prestel, 2001

Hunt, Peter (ed.), *The Shell Gardens Book*, Phoenix, 1964

Huxley, Anthony, *An Illustrated History of Gardening*, Paddington Press, 1978
Johnson, George, *A History of English Gardening*, Baldwin and Cradock, 1829
M'Intosh, Charles, *The Book of the Garden*, William Blackwood, 1853
Morris, Alistair, *Antiques from the Garden*, Art Press, 1999
Simmonds, A., *Horticultural Who was Who*, Royal Horticultural Society, 1948
Strong, Roy, *The Renaissance Garden in England*, Thames and Hudson, 1979
Thacker, Christopher, *The History of Gardens*, Croom Helm, 1979
Uglow, Jenny, *A Little History of British Gardening*, Pimlico, 2005
Webber, Ronald, *The Early Horticulturists*, David & Charles, 1968

Useful Websites

Best garden links – www.bestgardenlinks.co.uk
British wildflower plants – www.wildflowers.co.uk
Chelsea Flower Show – www.rhs.org.uk/chelsea
Chelsea Physic Garden – www.chelseaphysicgarden.co.uk
Chronological history – www.library.thinkquest.org
English wine – www.english-wine.com
English wine producers – www.englishwineproducers.com
Environment Agency – www.environment-agency.gov.uk.
The European Squirrel Initiative – www.europeansquirrelinitiative.org
Garden guides – www.gardenguides.com
Garden history links – www.magma.ca/~evb/garden.html
Garden History Society – www.gardenhistorysociety.org
Garden history – www.hcs.ohio-state.edu/hor/history
Garden Organic – www.gardenorganic.org.uk
Garden visits – www.gardenvisit.com
Garden Web – www.gardenweb.com
Gardening.com – www.gardening.com
Global Invasive Species Database – www.invasivespecies.net
Hedgeline – www.hedgeline
Historic Houses Association – www.hha.org.uk
Historic parks and gardens – www.york.ac.uk
Introduced species – www.introduced-species.co.uk
Japanese Knotweed Alliance – www.cabi.bioscience.org
Mammal Society – www.mammal.org.uk
National Gardens Scheme – www.ngs.org.uk.
Natural History Museum – www.nhm.ac.uk

National Vine Collection – http://vinenursery.netfirms.com
Plantlife – www.plantlife.org.uk
Plants that have changed history – www.killerplants.com
Rachel Carson Council – www.rachelcarson.org
Royal Botanic Gardens, Kew – www.rbgkew.org.uk
Royal Horticultural Society – www.rhs.org.uk
Stately Homes – www.statelyhomes.com
Talking plants – www.talkingplants.com
Topiary Organisation – www.topiary.org.uk
Top-selling garden tools – www.gardenideas.com
Victorian web – www.victorianweb.org
The Woodland Trust – www.woodland-trust.org

Chapter 1. Techno Wizards

Edwin Budding's Lawnmower

Bell, Brian, *Ransomes, Sims and Jefferies*, Old Pond, 2001
Cooksey, J.C.B., *Alexander Nasmyth, 1785–1840*, Lomond, 1991
Halford, David, *Old Lawn Mowers*, Shire, 1982
Hall, Andrew, 'The History of the Lawn Mower, 1830–1900', *Farm & Horticultural Equipment Collector*, Jan./Feb. 1995, pp. 6–7 and Mar./Apr. 1995, pp. 12–13
Baren, Maurice, *How it all Began in the Garden*, Smith Settle, 1994
Papworth, J.B., *Hints on Ornamental Gardening*, Papworth, 1823
Patent Office, Patent 5990, 31 August 1830, Budding
Sanecki, K.N., *Old Garden Tools*, Shire, 1979

John Aitken's Chainsaw

Bell, Brian, *Fifty Years of Garden Machinery*, Farming Press, 1995
Brown, James, *The Forester*, William Blackwood, 1894
Brown, Nelson Courtlandt, *Logging – Principles and Practices in the United States and Canada*, John Wiley, 1934
Grimshaw, Robert, *Saws*, Claxton, Remsen and Haffelfinger, 1880
Huggard, E., and Owen, T., *Forest Tools and Instruments*, Black, 1960
Skippen, Mark, Kikup, John, Maxton, Ronald, and McDonald, Stuart, 'The Chain Saw – A Scottish Invention', *Scottish Medical Journal* 49/2 (2004), 57–60
Spencer, H., *The History of British Midwifery from 1650 to 1800*, Bale, 1927
Wardrop, Jim, 'British Columbia's Experience with Early Chain Saws', *Stationary Engine* (January 1989), 5–7

Heron of Alexandria's Fountains

Bennet, Woodcroft (ed.), *The Pneumatics of Hero of Alexandria*, Taylor, Walton and Maberly, 1851

Caus, Salomon de, *Les Raison de Forces Mouuantes*, Norton, 1615

Coffin, David R., *Pirro Ligorio: The Renaissance Artist, Architect, and Antiquarian*, Pennsylvania State University Press, 2004

Hall, Marie Boas, *The Pneumatics of Hero of Alexandria*, Macdonald, 1971

Jellicoe, Geoffrey (*et al.*), *The Oxford Companion to Gardens*, Oxford University Press, 1991

Jellicoe, Susan, *Water: The Use of Water in Landscape Architecture*, Adam and Charles Black, 1971

MacDougall, Elisabeth Blair, *Fountains, Statues and Flowers*, Dumbarton Oaks Research Library, 1994

MacDougall, Elisabeth, and Miller, Naomi, *Fons Sapientiae*, Dumbarton Oaks, 1977

Mancini, Gioacchino, *Hadrian's Villa and Villa D'Este*, Old Vicarage, 1989

Montaigne, Michael de, *The Diary of Montaigne's Journey to Italy in 1580 and 1581*, Woolf, 1929

Switzer, Stephen, *An Introduction to a General System of Hydrostaticks and Hydraulicks*, Astley, 1729

Symmes, Marilyn, *Fountains, Splash and Spectacle*, Rizzoli, 1998

Percy Thrower, the Media Presenter

Bucknell, Barry, *Do-it-Yourself in the Garden*, Arco, 1965

Du Boulay, Shirley, *The Gardeners*, Hodder & Stoughton, 1985

Hadfield, B., Harling, R., and Highton, L., *British Gardeners*, Zwemmer, 1980, p. 285

The Independent, 19 March 1988

O'Sullivan, Timothy, *Percy Thrower: A Biography*, Sidgwick & Jackson, 1989

Thrower, Percy, *Picture Book of Gardening*, Collingridge, 1961

——, *My Lifetime of Gardening*, Hamlyn, 1977

The Times, 19 March 1988

Thomas Church's Timber Decking

Brookes, John, *Room Outside*, Thames and Hudson, 1969

Church, Thomas, *Your Private World*, Chronicle, 1969

——, *Gardens Are for People*, McGraw-Hill, 1983

Harris, Diane, 'Thomas Church as author: publicity and the professional at mid-century', *Studies in the History of Gardens and the Designed Landscape*, April–June, 2000

Laurie, Michael, *An Introduction to Landscape Architecture*, Elsevier, 1975

Messenger, Pam-Anela, 'El Novillero Revisited', *Landscape Design* (April 1983), 33–5

Punch, Walter (ed.), *Keeping Eden: A History of Gardening in America*, Bullfinch, 1992

Simo, Melanie, 'Regionalism and Modernism', in *Punch* (ed.), *Keeping Eden*

Treib, Marc (ed.), *An Everyday Modernism: The Houses of William Wurster*, San Francisco Museum of Modern Art, 1995

Caius Martius's Ornate Hedging

Blomfield, Reginald, and Thomas, F. Inig, *The Formal Garden in England*, Macmillan, 1892

Clevely, A.M., *Topiary: The Art of Clipping*, Salem House, 1988

Coats, Alice Margaret, *Garden Shrubs and Their Histories*, Vista, 1963

Colonna, Francesco, *Hypnerotomachia*, Venetiis, 1499

Curtis, C., and Gibson, W., *The Book of Topiary*, John Lane, 1904

Edwards, Paul, *English Garden Ornament*, Bell & Sons, 1965

Estienne, Charles, *Maison Rustique, or, The Countrey Farme*, John Bill, 1616

Hadfield, Miles, *Topiary and Ornamental Hedges*, Black, 1971

Leithart, Peter J., 'The Politics of Gratitude', *First Things* (December 2004)

Lloyd, Nathaniel, *Garden Craftsmanship in Yew and Box*, Ernest Benn, 1925

Sedding, John, *Garden-craft, Old and New*, Kegan Paul, 1891

Wolkomir, Richard, 'From "woody" to "stuffed" to shear madness, it's topiary', *Smithsonian*, 23/12 (March 1993), 100–9

Chapter 2. Garden Spoilers

Charles Isham's Gnomes

Bailey, Bruce, 'Sir Charles Edmund Isham', *ODNB*, 2004, pp. 426–7

Bartholomew, James, *Yew and Non-Yew*, Century, 1996

Behrens, Georg, *The Natural History of Hartz-Forest*, T. Osborne, 1730

Doyle, Arthur Conan, *The History of Spiritualism*, Cassell, 1926

Elliott, Brent, 'Gnomenclature', *The Garden* (April 1992), 172–5

——, *The Royal Horticultural Society: A History 1804–2004*, Phillimore, 2004

Geddes-Brown, Leslie, *The Royal Horticultural Society Chelsea*, Dorling Kindersley, 2000

Pavord, Anna, 'A home for a gnome', *Observer* (May 1988), 54–5

Pope, Alexander, *The Rape of the Lock*, Pope, 1712

Russell, Vivian, *Gnomes*, Frances Lincoln, 2005

Christopher Leyland's Monster Tree

Haslam, Richard, 'Leighton Hall Estate, Powys', *Country Life*, 17 June 1991, 116–19

Kew Bulletin, No. 3, 1926, 113–15

Mitchell, Alan, *The Gardener's Book of Trees*, Dent, 1991

Naylor, T.H., *The Family of Naylor from 1589*, Naylor, 1967

Osborn, A., 'An Interesting Hybrid Conifer', *Journal of the Royal Horticultural Society*, 66 (1941), 54–5

Ovens, H., Blight, W., and Mitchell, A., 'The Clones of Leyland Cypress', *Quarterly Journal of Forestry*, 58 (January 1964), 8–19

Slinn, Joy, *A Souvenir History of Haggerston Castle*, Brownlamb, 1995

William Harcourt's Country House Demolitions

Aslet, Clive, *The Last Country Houses*, Yale University Press, 1982

Elliott, Brent, *The Country House Garden: From the Archives of 'Country Life', 1897–1939*, Antique Collectors Club, 1995

English Heritage, *Register of Parks and Gardens of Special Historic Interest*, English Heritage, 1998

Harris, John, 'Heritage and Loss', in Strong, Binney and Harris, *The Destruction of the Country House*

Lees-Milne, James, *People and Places: Country House Donors and the National Trust*, John Murray, 1992

Stansky, Peter, *Ambitions and Strategies*, Clarendon Press, 1964

——, 'Harcourt, Sir William', *Oxford Dictionary of National Biography* (ODNB), Oxford University Press, 2005, pp. 138–43

Strong, Roy, *Country Life 1897–1997: The English Arcadia*, Country Life Books, 1996

Strong, R., Binney, M., and Harris, J., *The Destruction of the Country House, 1875–1975*, Thames and Hudson, 1974

Thomas, Graham Stuart, *Gardens of the National Trust*, Weidenfeld & Nicolson, 1979

University of Oxford, *Harcourt Arboretum: Restoration and Development Plan*, Botanic Garden, April 2003

Paul Muller's DDT Insecticide

Carson, Rachel, *Silent Spring*, Riverside Press, 1962
Elliott, Brent, *The Royal Horticultural Society: A History*, Phillimore, 2004
Hills, Lawrence D., *Pest Control Without Poisons*, Henry Doubleday Research Association, 1964
Mastalerz, Przemyslaw, *The True Story of DDT, PCB and Dioxin*, Wydawnictwo Chemiczne, 2005
Platt, Hugh, *The Jewel House of Art and Nature*, Bernard Alsop, 1653
Van den Bosch, Robert, *The Pesticide Conspiracy*, Prism Press, 1980
Wilson, George Fox, *The Detection and Control of Garden Pests*, Crosby Lockwood, 1947

John Innes's Peat Compost

Bellamy, David, *The Wild Boglands: Bellamy's Ireland*, Christopher Helm, 1986
Goodman, Judy, *John Innes and the Birth of Merton Park*, The John Innes Society, 1998
Howell, Graham, *Gardening Without Peat*, Friends of the Earth, 1991
Lawrence, William, *The Fruit, the seed and the soil*, Oliver & Boyd, 1954
——, *Catch the Tide*, Grower Books, 1980
MacGuire, Frances, and Elster, Jake, *Last Chance to See*, Friends of the Earth, 2001
Pollock, Mike, 'Peat and the gardener – an update', *The Garden*, 118/10 (October 1993), 454–7
RSPB, *Out of the Mire*, RSPB, 1993
West, Jenny, 'Innes, John', *ODNB*, 2004, pp. 303–4
Wilkinson, William, *Commission of Inquiry into Peat and Peatlands*, Plantlife, 1992

Chapter 3. Invaders and Infiltrators

Conrad Loddiges's Rhododendron

Elliott, Brent, 'Rhododendrons in British Gardens', in Postan, Cynthia (ed.), *The Rhododendron Story*, Royal Horticultural Society, 1996, pp. 156–86

Hackney Environmental Services, *Loddiges Nursery Hackney*, Hackney Council, n.d.

Hamilton, R.M., *Orchideae in the Collection of Conrad Loddiges*, Hamilton, 1991

Hibberd, Shirley, *The Amateur's Flower Garden*, London, 1871

Magor, E.W.M., 'The beginnings of rhododendron growing and hybridisation in Britain', *Rhododendrons* (1986–7), 27–32

Mills, Lawrence, 'Rhododendrons: the early history of their introduction and cultivation in Britain', *Rhododendrons* (1979–80), 6–20

Robinson, William, *The Wild Garden*, London, 1870

Robson, M., 'The Ponticum problem', *Rhododendrons* (1991), 46–9

Solman, David, *Loddiges of Hackney: The Largest Hothouse in the World*, Hackney Society Publication, 1995

Tabbush, P.M., '*Rhododendron ponticum* as a Forest Weed', *Forestry Commission Bulletin*, 73 (1987), 1–7

Emilio Levier's Giant Hogweed

Bingham, I.J., *Giant Hogweed: The Problem and its Control*, Scottish Agricultural Colleges, 1989

Environment Agency, *Guidance for the control of invasive plants near watercourses*, Environment Agency, 1996

Guinness World Records, *Guinness World Records*, Time, Incorporated Home Entertainment, 2003

Levier, Emilio, *A Travers le Caucase*, Levier, 1905

Mabey, Richard, *Flora Britannica: the Concise Edition*, Chatto & Windus, 1998

Royal Society for Protection of Birds, *The Birds in Your Garden*, RSPB, 1970

Thomas Brocklehurst's Squirrels

Dutton, Charles, *The Red Squirrel: Redressing the Wrong*, European Squirrel Initiative, 2004

Gurnell, John and Pepper, H., *Conserving the Red Squirrel*, Research Information Note, Forestry Commission, 1991

Holme, Jessica, *The Red Squirrel*, Shire, 1989

Laidler, Keith, *Squirrels in Britain*, David and Charles, 1980

Mayle, B., Pepper, H., and Ferryman, M., *Controlling Grey Squirrel Damage to Woodlands*, Forestry Commission, April 2003

Shorten, Monica, *Grey Squirrels*, Sunday Times, 1962

Pepper, H., *Survey of Squirrels in Britain*, Forestry Authority, 1992

Porter, Val, *Beastly Nuisances: Coping with Garden Pests*, Robson, 2003

Philipp von Siebold's Japanese Knotweed

Child, Lois, and Wade, Max, *The Japanese Knotweed Manual*, Packard, 2000

Cooke, A.S., *Japanese Knotweed: Its Status as a Pest and its Control in Conservation Areas*, CSD, 1988

Cornwall Knotweed Forum, *Japanese Knotweed*, Cornwall County Council, N.D.

Environment Agency, *Guidance for the control of invasive plants near watercourses*, Environment Agency, 1996

Hawke, C., and Williamson, D., *Japanese knotweed in amenity areas*, Arboriculture Research Note, no. 106/96, Department of Environment, 1992

Mabey, Richard, *Flora Britannica: The Concise Edition*, Chatto & Windus, 1998

Robinson, William, *The English Flower Garden*, John Murray, 1907

'Siebold, Philipp Franz von', *The New RHS Dictionary of Gardening*, Vol. 4, Macmillan, 1992

Welsh Development Agency, *Model Specification for the Control of Japanese Knotweed*, Welsh Development Agency, 1994

Christine Buisman and Dutch Elm Disease

Arboricultural Association, *Elm Trees are Dying*, Worplesdon, 1975

Clouston, Brian, and Stansfield, Kathy (eds), *After the Elm*, Heinemann, 1979

Evelyn, John, *Sylva, or a Discourse of Forest Trees*, Martyn & Allestry, 1664

Gibbs, John, Brasier, Clive, and Webber, Joan, *Dutch Elm Disease in Britain*, Research Information 252, The Forestry Authority, September 1994

Gilpin, William, *Remarks on Forest Scenery*, Blamire, 1791

Hanson, M.W., *Essex Elm*, Essex Field Club, 1990

Holmes, Francis W., 'Seven Dutch Women Scientists', in Sticklen, Marion, and Sherald, James, *Dutch Elm Disease Research*, Springer-Verlag, 1993, pp. 9–15

Karnosky, David, 'Dutch Elm Disease', *Environmental Conservation*, 6/4 (Winter 1979), 311–22

Loudon, John Claudius, *Arboretum et Fruicetum Britannicum*, Loudon, 1838

Sticklen, Marian, and Sherald, James, *Dutch Elm Disease Research*, Springer-Verlag, 1993

Strouts, R., and Winter, T., *Diagnosis of Ill-health in Trees*, HMSO, 2000

Chapter 4. Of Greatest Advantage

John Rose's English Vines

Barty-King, Hugh, *A Tradition of English Wine* (Oxford Illustrated Press), 1977

Blanche, Henrey, *British Botanical and Horticultural Literature before 1800*, vol. 1, Oxford University Press, 1975

Jeffers, Robert (ed.), Introduction to John Rose's *The English Vineyard*

Miller, Philip, *The Gardener's Dictionary*, London, 1747

Pearkes, Gillian, *Vinegrowing in Britain*, Dent, 1982

Raphael, Sandra, 'John Rose', vol. 47, *ODNB*, 2004, pp. 761–2

Rose, John, *The English Vineyard Vindicated*, Herb Grower, 1965

Skelton, Stephen, *The Vineyards of England*, Skelton, 1989

Carolus Clusius's Flower Garden

Abbas, Barbara (*et al.*), *The Garden Book*, Phaidon Press, 2003

Anderson, A.W., *The Coming of the Flowers*, Williams and Norgate, 1900

Clusius, Carolus, *Rariorum plantarum historia*, Officina Plantiniana apud Ioannem Moretum, 1601

Dash, Mike, *Tulipomania*, Indigo, 2000

Hyams, Edward, and Macquitty, William, *Great Botanical Gardens of the World*, Nelson, 1969

Jellicoe, Geoffrey (*et al.*), *The Oxford Companion to Gardens*, Oxford University Press, 1991, pp. 67, 80–1, 122, 390–5

Menten, Theodore (ed.), *Plant and Floral Woodcuts for Designers and Craftsmen*, Dover, 1974

Pavord, Anna, *The Tulip*, Bloomsbury, 1999

Huxley, Anthony (ed.), *The New Royal Horticultural Society Dictionary of Gardening*, Macmillan, 1992, pp. 658–9

Schama, Simon, *The Embarrassment of Riches*, Fontana, 1988

Van Dijk, W. (ed.), *A Treatise on Tulips*, Associated Bulb Growers of Holland, 1951

John Loudon's Horticultural Journal

Boniface, Priscilla (ed.), *In Search of English Gardens*, Century, 1987

Desmond, R., 'Loudon and Nineteenth-Century Horticultural Journalism', in MacDougall, Elisabeth (ed.), *John Claudius Loudon and the Early Nineteenth Century in Great Britain* (Dumbarton Oaks, 1980), pp. 77–109

Elliott, Brent, *The Country House Garden: From the Archives of 'Country Life' 1897–1939*, Antique Collectors Club, 1995

——, 'Loudon, John Claudius', *ODNB*, 2004, pp. 474–7

The *Gardener's Magazine*, vol. 1, 1826

Gloag, John, *Mr Loudon's England*, Oriel, 1970

Jellicoe, G. (*et al.*), *The Oxford Companion to Gardens*, Oxford University Press, 1991, pp. 212–13, 457–8
Loudon, John, *An Encyclopaedia of Gardening*, Longman, 1841 and 1860
——, *Self-instruction for Young Gardeners*, Longman, 1847
Simo, Melanie, *Loudon and the Landscape*, Yale University Press, 1988
Taylor, Geoffrey, *Some Nineteenth Century Gardeners*, Skeffington, 1951

Martin Hope Sutton's Packet Seeds

Baren, Maurice, *How it all Began in the Garden*, Smith Settle, 1994
Corley, Tony, 'The making of a Berkshire entrepreneur', *Berkshire Archaeological Journal*, 74 (1991–3), 135–43
——, 'A Berkshire entrepreneur makes good', *Berkshire Archaeological Journal*, 75 (1994–7), 103–10
——, 'A Berkshire entrepreneur's final years', *Berkshire Archaeological Journal*, 76 (1998–2003), 94–101
Cheales, Alan, *MHS*, printed privately, 1898
Hodder, T.K., 'Sutton's at Reading', *The Journal of the Royal Horticultural Society*, Vol. 81, part 5, May 1956, 1–8
Sutton & Sons, *Sutton's Amateur's Guide in Horticulture*, Sutton & Sons, 1877
Sutton & Sons, *Sutton's Royal Seed Establishment at Reading*, Sutton & Sons, 1907

Harry Veitch's Chelsea Flower Show

Baigent, Elizabeth, 'Sir Harry James Veitch', *ODNB*, 2004, pp. 234–5
Elliott, Brent, *The Royal Horticultural Gardens: A History 1804–2004*, Phillimore, 2004
Fletcher, Harold, *The Story of the Royal Horticultural Society*, Oxford University Press, 1969
Geddes-Brown, Leslie, *The Royal Horticultural Society Chelsea: The Greatest Flower Show on Earth*, Dorling Kindersley, 2004
Hadfield, B., Harling, R., and Highton, L., *British Gardeners: A Biographical Dictionary*, Zwemmer, 1980, pp. 31–2, 296
Jellicoe, G. (*et al.*), *The Oxford Companion to Gardens*, Oxford University Press, 1991, pp. 487, 582
Joyce, David (ed.), *The Chelsea Year 1988/9*, Chatto & Windus, 1988
Marsden-Smedley, Hester, *The Chelsea Flower Show*, Constable, 1976
Moore, Susan, 'Pictures of a Horticulturalist', *Country Life*, 28 May 1981
Morison, Patricia, 'Chelsea Flower Show', *Daily Telegraph*, 23 May 1988

Shephard, Sue, *Seeds of Fortune*, Bloomsbury, 2003
Veitch, James Herbert, *Hortus Veitchii*, Veitch, 1906

Elsie Wagg's National Gardens Scheme

Johnson, Judy, Berry, Susan, and Wooster, Steven, *English Private Gardens Open to the Public in aid of the National Gardens Scheme*, Collins & Brown, 1991
'The National Memorial to Queen Alexandra', *Country Life*, 18 June 1927, 986–93
Elliott, Brent, *The Country House Garden: From the Archives of 'Country Life', 1897–1939*, Antique Collectors Club, 1995
Hunningher, Erica, *A Nurturing Nature: The Story of the National Gardens Scheme*, Museum of Garden History, 2001
Hunningher, Erica (ed.), *Making Gardens*, Cassell, 2001
Hussey, Christopher, *English Country Houses Open to the Public*, Country Life, 1951
Leppard, M.J., *A History of East Grinstead*, Phillimore, 2001
Rix, Martyn and Alison, *Garden Open Today*, Viking, 1987
Thomas, Graham Stuart, *Gardens of the National Trust*, Weidenfeld & Nicolson, 1979

Mini Histories

James Sharp's Metal Roller, p. 13

Morris, Alister, *Antiques From the Garden*, Garden Art Press, 1999
Sanecki, K.N., *Old Garden Tools*, Shire, 1979

Edward Stewart's Garden Centre, p. 42

Du Boulay, Shirley, *The Gardeners*, Hodder & Stoughton, 1985

John Manning's Prefab Shed, p. 87

Sloan, Samuel, *American Houses*, Philadelphia, 1861

Guillaume Beaumont's Ha-ha, p. 96

Fleming, Laurence and Gore, Alan, *The English Garden*, Michael Joseph, 1979

Lawerence Hills' Organic Movement, p. 110

Hills, Lawrence, *Down to Earth Fruit and Vegetable Growing*, Faber & Faber, 1960
——, *Pest Control without Poisons*, Henry Doubleday Research Association, 1964
——, *Down to Earth Gardening*, Faber & Faber, 1967

Richard Bradley's Water Plants Tub, p. 129

Bradley, Richard, *New Improvements of Planting and Gardening*, Mears, 1717
Jellicoe, Geoffrey (*et al.*), *The Oxford Companion to Gardens* Oxford University Press, 1991, p. 536
Huxley, Anthony, *An Illustrated History of Gardening*, Paddington, 1978

Princess Augusta's Gardens at Kew, p. 138

Hadfield, M., Harling, R., and Highton L., *British Gardeners*, Zwemmer, 1980
Kew Gardens publication, *The Royal Botanic Gardens Kew*, HMSO, 1954

Bridges Adams' Rooftop Terrace, p. 165

Le Lievre, Audrey, 'Gardens Among the Chimneypots', *Country Life*, March 1989, 120–1
Adams, W. Bridges, 'How to Convert London into a Garden', *Once a Week*, 1 (17 Dec. 1859), 519–22

Index

Index

Index

Index